Casey,

# DRINKING

## THE

# DEVIL'S ACRE

A LOVE LETTER from SAN FRANCISCO and HER COCKTAILS

**DUGGAN McDONNELL**

Photographs by Luke Abiol

Always, drink it in!

CHRONICLE BOOKS

SAN FRANCISCO

Library of Congress Cataloging-in-Publication Data:

McDonnell, Duggan.

Drinking the devil's acre : a love letter from San Francisco and her cocktails / Duggan McDonnell ; photographs by Luke Abiol.

pages cm

Includes bibliographical references and index.

ISBN 978-1-4521-3525-0

1. Cocktails. 2. Bars (Drinking establishments)—California— San Francisco—History. I. Abiol, Luke. II. Title.


TX951.M3465 2015

641.87'4—dc23

2014044040


Manufactured in China

Designed by Public, SF

Archival photographs: SAN FRANCISCO HISTORY CENTER, SAN FRANCISCO PUBLIC LIBRARY

Photograph on page 175, © Moulin Studios

Photograph on page 250, "Vue panoramique de San Francisco" by Louis-Philippe Breault - Own work. Licensed under CC BY-SA 3.0 via Wikimedia Commons.

10 9 8 7 6 5 4 3 2

Chronicle Books LLC

680 Second Street

San Francisco, California 94107

www.chroniclebooks.com

This book is dedicated to everyone everywhere
who has ever enjoyed a cocktail in San Francisco.
You're always welcome to visit us again,
to step inside our doors, sit on our bar stools,
and imbibe away the joys of the day.

*Louis Parentis' Saloon located on Pacific Street, February 15, 1934*

# A CHRONOLOGY OF
## COCKTAILS, DISTILLED SPIRITS, EPISTLES, AND EVENTS OF THE BARBARY COAST

**1579** Sir Francis Drake sails into a cove (now known as Drake's Bay) just north of the Golden Gate after sacking the port of Pisco, Peru, and pillaging three hundred *botijas* of prized Pisco. Drake and his merry men spend six weeks of respite concocting what may be the world's first cocktail.

**1776** Spain controls Alta California, part of the Viceroyalty of New Spain, and Franciscan missionaries arrive in San Francisco to found Misión San Francisco de Asís, colloquially known as Mission Dolores. A short time later, the missions at San Jose and Sonoma are founded, vineyards are planted, and the first spirit of California, *aguardiente de vino* (later called Pisco and then brandy), produced from the Mission grape, is distilled.

**1847** "Punch Drinking and Its Effects," the first piece of fiction to appear in California's first newspaper, the *Californian*, is published.

**1848** Gold is discovered at Sutter's Mill in the Sierra Nevada foothills.

**1851** The Old Ship Saloon, today San Francisco's oldest (continuously operating) house of drink, opened its doors for business at what is now 298 Pacific Avenue.

**1857–62** "Professor" Jerry Thomas tends bar at the Occidental Hotel, San Francisco, where he earns a better salary than the vice president of the United States. In 1862, he publishes *How to Mix Drinks, or The Bon-Vivant's Companion*, the world's first treatise to curate cocktail recipes, mixology, and spirits.

**1860**      For the first time, the term *Barbary Coast* is used to describe a specific and notorious forty-square-block area in the northwestern corner of San Francisco.

**1864**      Samuel Clemens arrives in San Francisco, begins his writing career for the *Daily Morning Call*, using the nom de plume Mark Twain.

**1867**      Charles Campbell publishes *The American Bar-keeper*.

**1882**      Harry Johnson publishes his *New and Improved Bartender's Manual*.

**1891**      *Cocktail Boothby's American Bar-Tender* by "Cocktail Bill" Boothby is published.

**1893**      Duncan Nicol becomes proprietor of the Bank Exchange Saloon and perfectly promotes the infamous house cocktail, the Pisco punch.

**1904**      May E. Southworth publishes her *One Hundred and One Beverages*.

**1906**      The earthquake and ensuing fire strike and consume much of San Francisco. Among the surviving structures is the Hotaling warehouse, where much of the city's distilled spirits are stored.

**1917**      The San Francisco Police Department blockades, then raids, the Barbary Coast district, permanently closing eighty-three brothels and forty saloons all within its forty-block boundary.

**1919–33** The years of Prohibition.

**1933**      *The Barbary Coast: An Informal History of the San Francisco Underworld* by Herbert Asbury is published.

**1934**      Victor "The Trader" Bergeron opens his first restaurant, Hinky Dinks, in Oakland, which soon morphs into his eponymous Trader Vic's.

**1937**      *Liquid Gems* is published by John R. Iverson.

**1939**      *The Time of Your Life*, William Saroyan's Pulitzer Prize–winning play set in "a saloon on San Francisco's Pacific Street," is produced on Broadway for the first time.

**1941**      San Francisco's *Hocker's Alcoholic Beverage Encyclopedia* is published by Curtis Hocker.

**1943**      The city's first farmers' market opens on Alemany Boulevard.

**1948**      Vesuvio Cafe opens its doors and soon becomes the well-oiled hub of the beatniks, a term coined a decade later by famed *San Francisco Chronicle* columnist Herb Caen.

**1952**      The first Irish coffee is poured at the Buena Vista Café, Fisherman's Wharf.

**1965**      Tommy's Mexican Restaurant opens in the Richmond District.

**1971**      Harry Denton begins tending bar at Henry Africa's on Polk Street, the world's first fern bar.

               *Pour Man's Friend: A Guide and Reference for Bar Personnel* by John C. Burton is published.

**1981**      The Wine Appreciation Guild publishes *California Brandy Drinks*.

**1982**      St. George Spirits begins distilling eau-de-vie in Emeryville.

**1983**      Charbay Winery & Distillery, yet another pioneering operation in the artisanal spirits movement, opens in Napa.

**1994**      Fritz Maytag and the team of Anchor Brewing distill their first batch of American rye whiskey in San Francisco.

**1996**      The Starlight Room, led by barman Tony Abou-Ganim, opens atop the Sir Francis Drake Hotel in downtown San Francisco.

**1998**      Absinthe Brasserie & Bar opens its doors with its famous neoclassic cocktail program led by Marco Dionysos.

               Paul Harrington's *Cocktail: The Drinks Bible for the 21st Century* is published.

**2000**    Gary "Gaz" Regan publishes his first column on cocktails in the *San Francisco Chronicle*.

**2002**    Jordan Mackay begins writing on spirits and cocktails for *7x7* magazine. Alcademics, CHOW, and other media outlets start extensively covering the renaissance of cocktail culture in the Bay Area.

**2004**    After decades of inactivity, the United States Bartender's Guild is relaunched in San Francisco.

**2005**    *The Art of the Bar: Cocktails Inspired by the Classics* by Jeff Hollinger and Robert Schwartz is published.

Distillery No. 209 begins distilling gin in San Francisco.

**2006**    The world's first farmers' market cocktail event, organized by Square One Organic vodka and CUESA, is held at the San Francisco Ferry Building.

**2007**    Guillermo Toro-Lira's *Wings of Cherubs: The Saga of the Rediscovery of Pisco Punch, Old San Francisco's Mystery Drink* is published.

San Francisco Cocktail Week is conceived and produced by H. Joseph Ehrmann, Jeff Hollinger, and Duggan McDonnell.

**2009**    *Artisanal Cocktails* by Scott Beattie is published, and *DrinkMe* and *Mutineer* magazines are founded.

Liquor.com is launched from San Francisco onto the global Web landscape.

**2010**    *Left Coast Libations* by Michael Lazar and Ted Munat is published.

Pisco, the first spirit imbibed in California, returns with a vigor via the locally owned brand Campo de Encanto, as well as other labels, produced in Peru.

*Broadway at Kearny, 1929*

*The center of sin in San Francisco was the diagonally cut block bounded by Broadway, Kearny, and Montgomery Streets—a comparatively small area, but so reeking with depravity that it was known both to the police and to its habitués as the Devil's Acre. In its issue of February 28, 1886, the* San Francisco Call *described it as "the resort and abiding place of the worst criminals in town," and complained that respectable citizens could not traverse Kearny Street on their way to and from business without witnessing "the utter shamelessness of the denizens". . . . It was the particular rendezvous of the pimps and of the lush-workers who thronged the Devil's Acre; that is, thieves who specialized in robbing drunken men, having first, if necessary, knocked them unconscious with a slug or section of lead pipe. The Morgue (a Saloon) was also headquarters for the many drug addicts, better known in those days as hoppies, who lived in the alleys of Chinatown and the Barbary Coast.*

—HERBERT ASBURY, *The Barbary Coast: An Informal History of the San Francisco Underground*

# CONTENTS

**Preface.... 16**

**Introduction.... 25**

No. 1: The Martinez.... 37

No. 2: The Mai Tai.... 53

No. 3: The Pisco Punch.... 63

No. 4: The Highball.... 73

No. 5: The Negroni.... 77

No. 6: The Irish Coffee.... 85

No. 7: The Scorpion Bowl.... 93

No. 8: The Manhattan.... 99

No. 9: The Bloody Mary.... 111

No. 10: The Sidecar.... 117

No. 11: The Mojito.... 125

**1,001 NIGHTS BEHIND BARS.... 133**

No. 12: The Margarita.... 143

No. 13: The Sazerac.... 151

No. 14: The French 75.... 155

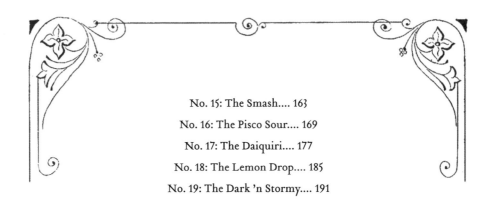

No. 15: The Smash.... 163

No. 16: The Pisco Sour.... 169

No. 17: The Daiquiri.... 177

No. 18: The Lemon Drop.... 185

No. 19: The Dark 'n Stormy.... 191

**THE BARBARY COAST BARKEEP.... 198**

No. 20: The Ginger Rogers.... 203

No. 21: The Blood and Sand.... 207

No. 22: The Sangria.... 213

**HETCH HETCHY'S PURE WATER
AND THE ICE IN EVERY SAN FRANCISCAN COCKTAIL.... 217**

No. 23: The Chartreuse Swizzle.... 221

No. 24: The Basil Gimlet.... 227

**THE HANDS THAT TASTE.... 231**

No. 25: The Laughing Buddha.... 235

**To Create Every Cocktail with Love.... 238**

**To Hold the Past in the Future.... 240**

**San Francisco Cocktail Route.... 247**

**Recommended Reading.... 248**

**Acknowledgments.... 251**

**Index.... 252**

*Saloon of Wheeland & Collins, St. Francis Hotel, March 22, 1933*

# PREFACE

*It is more fun to be sick in California
than to be well anywhere else.*

—INEZ HAYNES IRWIN, *The Californiacs*

San Francisco, born from a womb of gold, came into the world as a celebratory, multi-cultural, altogether combustible boomtown. It arose overnight out of Latin America and established its own identity distinct from the rest of the country, albeit with a warm, congenial desire for community. California, as part of Spain and then Mexico, had been Roman Catholic territory, which was heavily reliant on the liturgy of the sacrament; drinking wine was already an important part of its culture. Franciscan fathers introduced vineyards in the late 1700s; wineries, which were simultaneously distilleries for *aguardiente de vino*—later known colloquially as Pisco and still later as brandy—were built; and alcohol, whether for ritual or recreational purposes, became essential to the daily lives of Californians.

When the rush for gold arrived in the mid-1800s, millions of dollars flowed into San Francisco, and the city soon boasted more saloons per capita than any other city in the world. By 1859, it had become one of the largest municipalities in the country. The weather offered a perfect drinker's climate; to sally into a cocktail saloon kept the fortune seeker safe from wind and fog, and a brandy smash never failed to warm the chest. With so much money to burn and with so few persons with an extended family around for whom they might otherwise have to behave, the easygoing, wine-drinking culture of Latin America shed its old skin, and San Francisco became the wildest place on Earth. Not surprisingly, an incredibly racially diverse population soon put down roots in the lively port; and instantly, cross-cultural commerce and intermarriage began. Decades later, the Anti-Saloon League hardly caught on in San Francisco, and during Prohibition, the Noble Experiment wasn't especially enforced.

No other city in the world grew up as fast, as rich, as tolerant, and as vibrant as San Francisco. And the cocktail was there from Day One: in a Martinez, a California milk punch, or the gold rush–era Sazerac, we discover the fresh, celebratory, innovative character of San Francisco—a culture culled from ports around the world.

Infamous for its concentration of saloons, dance halls, and other delights, the Barbary Coast was a forty-square-block area in the northeast corner of the city that in 1890 boasted "the right to sell beer, whisky and other intoxicating beverages to 3,117 places, or one for every ninety-six inhabitants," scribbled the historian of America's underworld, Herbert Asbury, in *The Barbary Coast*. "And there were at least two thousand blind pigs, or blind tigers, as speakeasies were called in those days, which operated without licenses." By comparison, the population of San Francisco today is nearly three times greater than it was in 1890, with only 1,179 pouring liquor licenses as of this writing, or one outlet of cocktail pleasure for every seven hundred persons. How many blind tigers are in operation remains unknown, of course.

Given the numbers, the Barbary Coast was clearly not the place where bartenders curated a menu of signature cocktails, that is, unless the guest was looking for a signature Mickey Finn: diluted whiskey, adulterated with prune juice to falsify aging, infused with chiles to give some kick, and then spiked with opium to knock a fella out! According to hyperbolic accounts of history, this wilderness even boasted a saloon that held drinking contests in which a grizzly bear chained in the middle of the barroom was pitted against men to see who could consume more milk punch! In *Lights and Shades in San Francisco*, published in 1876, Benjamin Lloyd wrote that the "Barbary Coast is the haunt of the low and the vile of every kind. The petty thief, the house burglar, the tramp, the whoremonger, lewd women, cut-throats, murderers, all are found here. Dance-halls and concert saloons, where blear-eyed men and faded women drink vile liquor, smoke offensive tobacco, engage in vulgar conduct, sing obscene songs and say and do everything to heap upon themselves more degradation, are numerous. Low gambling houses, thronged with riot-loving rowdies, in all stages of intoxication, are there. Licentiousness, debauchery, pollution, loathsome disease, insanity from dissipation, misery, poverty, wealth, profanity, blasphemy, and death, are there. And Hell, yawning to receive the putrid mass, is there also."

The title of Devil's Acre comes from the name of a little island bordered by three streets, a triangular burg that was once the wickedest, wildest single block in the whole of the world and the backbone of the Barbary Coast. In the mid-twentieth century, it was the bars of the Devil's Acre that Kerouac and Cassady darted in and out of, languishing over wine spodiodi and whiskey of every sort to birth the Beat Generation. For nearly one hundred years, through multiple fires, earthquakes, police raids, and many a cultural renaissance, the Devil's Acre, Barbary Coast, San Francisco was one long romp of bottles popping, the whole of the world coming together in a den of vice and virtue. That's San Francisco!

* * *

In the cocktail class I've long taught, A History of San Francisco in Seven Cocktails, I reveal the dichotomy of forces at work in San Francisco's cocktail ancestry, from the earliest and best cocktail books published in the country to the City's most dangerous shanghaiing saloons. With every class, the three hours come and go quickly, and my students are always abuzz after their immersive experience of adding Champagne to a Manhattan to create the Boothby cocktail or of shaking a wonderfully crisp mai tai. Within those three hours, I share the legends and lore of how certain cocktails came to be, such as how the mojito, the world's first cocktail, was created in Northern California. It is these *cocktales*, their origins and the great how-to of cocktailing, that I rejoice in telling, and that's what you'll discover in these pages. What I endeavor to impress upon my students is not whether a cocktail was actually conceived within the City's borders; the significance is instead found in the City's embrace of a drink, of its ingredients and flavor, and in how a collection of cocktails can be seen as a portrait of a place.

You've likely noticed that when I refer to San Francisco as the City, it is always with a capital, an almost royal C. It's an expression of local parlance that I inherited from my father who inherited its use from his father who inherited the descriptor from his father before him, and so on. If you grew up within or near our uniquely Western, yet-oh-so-European city, or really, anywhere within the American West in the nineteenth or early twentieth century, San Francisco was the City, the only city. These days it's a bygone term of endearment, an expression of sentimental pride that links locals to their past. And because native pride fills every sentence within these pages, I refer to San Francisco as *the City*.

* * *

Cocktails are every bit as significant a cultural force and as deserving a part of San Francisco's historical narrative as food and wine, having unequivocally contributed to its culinary identity. San Francisco began as a city of drink, and from its infancy, discerning and decisive San Franciscans tippled by calling out the name of their drink. The City did not begin with the ribald Barbary Coast. Nor was it the Arizona or Colorado of the Wild West, where thirsty pioneers dumbly hollered "Whiskey!" No, this was the San Francisco of the gold rush, the Comstock Lode, a city shaped by the Big Four and other robber barons, and the prevailing culture spoke civilly to, rather than shouted at, the barkeep: "Whiskey smash, if you please." "Sherry cobbler, if you don't mind." "Claret and lemonade, if it's no trouble." "Pisco punch, and take your time." It wasn't a culture that barked for straight hooch. Instead, the tune sung throughout was of freshly squeezed citrus, sprigs of peppermint, and oh so many dashes of bitters.

San Francisco was famous for its cocktails long before it was known for its cuisine. The Bay Area is home to Chez Panisse and Michael Mina and legions of chefs knighted as celebrities thanks to television. California's first cookbook, *Vintage California Cuisine*, was published in 1889, but by then, San Francisco's drinking culture was already four decades old, and cocktails had been big business throughout those years, as evidenced by a lively publishing scene. Jerry Thomas's *How to Mix Drinks, or The Bon-Vivant's Companion* was issued in 1862; the surviving first editions of Harry Johnson's *New and Improved Bartender's Manual*, which appeared in 1882, all refer to an earlier 1850 edition (with the claim that the many thousands printed sold out immediately, then vanished from the earth); and in 1867, a Charles Campbell published *The American Bar-keeper*, though many believed that Charles Campbell was the nom de plume of a publisher out to capitalize on the rising trend of mixed drinks. Then, in 1891, "Cocktail Bill" Boothby published his *Cocktail Boothby's American Bar-Tender*. This amount of activity in such a small and young city leaves no doubt that, from the start, San Francisco took pride in great drink and the talent was always there to meet the demand. From 1849 on, the Port of San Francisco was busy embracing the finest wines and spirits the world had to offer, and her best and brightest barmen were only all too happy to showcase these delights on the printed page.

A climate of wind and fog, an economy built on gold, and a great natural harbor on the Pacific made San Francisco the perfect city in which to cocktail. We do not credit Paris with putting food on a plate first; we credit Paris with the advent of culinary cuisine. San Francisco should be similarly recognized for developing culinary cocktails. Punches, grogs, and cocktails of a passably drinking sort had long existed, but it was the cool air and all that gold that fueled the liquid inventions in San Francisco. The City created not only the drinks but also the culture in which drinking the finest concoctions at any hour, day or night, is de rigueur. The tradition of cocktailing was born in San Francisco exactly when the first bags of gold arrived from the Sierras, and it only grew stronger with more reigns of gold, including the first dot-com boom at the turn of the most recent century.

In *Everyone Eats: Understanding Food and Culture*, noted culinary anthropologist E. N. Anderson writes, "Food is used in every society on Earth to communicate messages. Preeminent among these are messages of group solidarity; food sharing is literally sacred in almost all religions and takes on a near-sacred quality in many (most?) families around the world. It also carries messages about status, gender, role, ethnicity, religion, identity, and other socially constructed regimes. It is also, very often, used in more fine-tuned ways to mark or indicate particular occasions, particular personal qualities, particular hangups or concerns. It is subject to snobbism, manipulation, and debate." Anderson is right, that's certain.

Let's apply Anderson's theory to cocktails, to San Francisco, and rewrite his statement: Cocktails are used in San Francisco to communicate messages. Preeminent among these are messages of group solidarity; the sharing of a drink is literally sacred in every neighborhood restaurant and tavern and takes on a near-sacred quality in many homes across its forty-nine square miles. The drinking of a particular cocktail also carries messages about status, gender, employment, ethnicity, religion, identity, and other socially constructed regimes. The choice of one's drink is then, very often, used in more fine-tuned ways, to mark or indicate particular occasions, particular personal qualities, particular hang-ups or concerns. And cocktails in The City are, as a matter of course, always subject to snobbism, interpretation, and debate. Now, that sounds like someone is talking about San Francisco!

* * *

San Francisco has a highly localized preference for cocktails and, within that, a unified preference for bright, bitter, and boozy on the palate. Residents appreciate drinks that sing in the glass, fresh with essential oils from muddled mint, hand-squeezed lime, or an expressed orange peel, pinched and then dropped into the glass. The Negroni is a perfect example of the San Francisco palate: equal parts dry gin, Italian vermouth, and Campari stirred, then strained into an ice-filled highball glass and garnished with a long orange peel. It is altogether bright, bitter, and boozy—notes of bittersweet grapefruit leap with undertones of baking spices, juniper, caramel, and grape. A Negroni thus serves as both aperitif and digestif—a cocktail for all occasions.

A predilection for bitter over sweet has long been the choice of the affluent. Bitter is thought to be better because it is an acquired taste, a component of a sophisticated society. San Francisco began as a culture of immediate affluence. Even when the streets were full of mud, there was opera. When men couldn't get their clothing properly cleaned, there was French fashion. Did San Francisco immediately have a preference for *amari*, or cocktail bitters? Perhaps. A Campari and soda was a popular cocktail in the City before World War II, and Campari has remained a staple. Is this because American soldiers were exposed to the culture of Europe while serving abroad and brought that taste back home? Or, can it be attributed to the heavy wave of immigration from northern Italy in the first decades of the twentieth century? Both are likely true.

Before this piece of land at the end of a peninsula between the Pacific and the bay became San Francisco de Asís, it was known as Yerba Buena, or "good herb," so named for the mint that flourished throughout the area. John Burton, a San Francisco native who began tending bar in 1959, told me that in his early days, "besides making fresh-squeezed sweet-and-sour mix every day, we picked fresh mint. Mint was the most important garnish because San Francisco has always loved its native herb." It's good to know that long before the current mojito craze, before barkeeps began to procure produce at a farmers' market for every shift, this beautiful and aromatic herb was a standard component of a bar's *mise en place*.

Fresh-squeezed citrus has been a part of Spanish American drinking culture for over four hundred years. As spirits were developed in the New World, beginning with Pisco, then with mezcal and rum, a lime seemed ever ready to squeeze into them. Father Junípero Serra planted the first citrus tree in California in 1769; nearly a century later, during the gold rush, oranges were cultivated in Southern California for shipping to mining camps to help combat scurvy. In 1873, the navel orange, a sweet, seedless clone of a mutation of a Brazilian sour orange, was cultivated for the first time in California. Later, mandarin oranges, such as the satsuma, and their close relatives, tangerines, were planted, as were Meyer and Eureka lemons. Limes came from Mexico, arriving at the Port of San Francisco from Puerta Vallarta. With so much access to citrus, it's no wonder that San Francisco loves the fruit and has long insisted on fresh-squeezed juices in its smashes, East Indias, sidecars, margaritas, mai tais, and more.

The enjoyment of delicious, intoxicating drinks is a quintessential human experience. The enjoyment of finer alcohols, however, is generally an urban, upper-class experience. In a city like San Francisco, where people expect a masterful curation of wines and spirits at all hours of the day, the economy of the City would nearly collapse without these refined spirits. And what sits atop the hierarchy as the finest and most imaginative way to enjoy a glass of something intoxicating? The cocktail, of course. Remove the shaking and stirring of cocktails from the urban landscape of San Francisco and you strip it of it of its blood and limbs, leaving it lifeless and cold.

Sure, New York will always provide cocktail's biggest stage. London holds the pure pluck and vigor that will always convince. Havana, too, had its heyday, and Paris remains a decadent sip of history. Honolulu, with its Blue Hawaii, has long offered intoxication garnished with an umbrella. New Orleans knows no town can compare to its nonstop Mardi Gras of liquid delight. But the talents of the sporting bar folk and the freshness of the cocktails in the San Francisco Bay Area remain true, having stayed steady since the days when the portly Jerry Thomas and the irrepressible young German American Harry Johnson reigned over the Barbary Coast, inventing and grandstanding, commanding the palates of the world's thirsty.

* * *

There is something noble about a chef preparing his or her grandmother's recipes, cooking the same dishes that were served in the home, dishes that sometimes originated in another country. This is cooking with a sense of place. Eating a dish in the spot where it was first created is also rewarding: a muffuletta at Central Grocery in New Orleans, crispy pork tenderloin sandwiches along the Iowa-Missouri border, a marionberry pie in Oregon. The United States is home to many great regional cuisines—areas where ingredients and dietary preferences reflect the geography and ethnic history. I hope that our culture stays that way, that regional culinary specialties remain unbent by modern trends of homogenization. Simply put, I don't want to eat Texas barbecue when I'm in North Carolina, and vice-versa.

A Ramos gin fizz tastes better when sipped in the French Quarter. A French 75 sipped inside Harry's New York Bar in Paris, where it first took shape, is incomparable. Fifteen years ago, the smartest cocktailians in America tripped down a set of stairs below Seattle's

Pike Place Market to find a small den of cocktail preservation where cult favorite Murray Stenson could be found exhuming and shaking such revitalized classics as the Last Word. The rite of passage in San Francisco means throwing back pitchers of margaritas at Tommy's, where they are made from 100 percent agave tequila, with but a nip of agave nectar and the freshest of limes, and are pitched back and forth by hand between dilapidated plastic pitchers—never shaken—by the proprietor, Julio Bermejo.

*Drinking the Devil's Acre*, then, isn't about that vague soup called pre-Prohibition cocktails, wherein all cocktails created before 1919 are lumped together regardless of their appellation and date of origin. (That retrospective bundling has only worsened in this Internet era.) This book is excited to concern itself with a specific place, and that place's specific beginning, and those specific tasty traditions—the cocktail habits of San Francisco, from Sir Francis Drake in 1579 up to this present moment of the cocktail renaissance. As I have acknowledged, there have been six great cocktail cities in the world: London and Havana, New York and Paris, New Orleans and San Francisco. Here I am focusing on the last one, variously known as Baghdad by the Bay, Yerba Buena, and Fog City. It is, of course, the youngest of the six cities, and it's also the only one whose streets were alive with great drink from its beginning.

What follows are twenty-five vignettes, each focused on a singular drink's story and significance to San Francisco. Within that context, I discuss each cocktail's ingredients, sharing the origins of gin, for example. And because these cocktails have in turn birthed other cocktails, I have also included a few additional recipes of local import that represent that phenomenon. None of these recipes is fussy or calls for an elaborate presentation based on obscure ingredients. Nothing in these pages strives to be avant-garde or trendy. Rather, they hold history and lore poured out by a man who gives a damn, and that fulcrum, folks, is always forward facing.

You'll find out who put the now-famous Pisco punch on the map, how San Francisco contributed to the Sazerac and the Pisco sour, and what the world's first cocktail was. Nineteenth-century saloon keeping was rife with recipes for doctoring booze to re-create the flavor of whiskey without actually pouring any whiskey. The first cocktail books, which were written for the trade, openly carried these formulas, as it was accepted that tradesmen would cheat consumers to make a little extra dough. Today's culture of transparency, along with the popularity of artisanal spirits and farmers' markets, has made such practices abhorrent. So, to benefit the bar and the guest, the mixologist and the cocktail groupie, I've turned that old custom on its head by revealing my formulas for blending cocktail whiskey, cocktail gin, cocktail blackstrap rum, and so on. My intent is to inspire you to become both mixologist and master blender.

Are these twenty-five drinks the most representative of the City itself, the real heart and soul of San Francisco? I think so. Is there one cocktail of the lot that stands out, rising above the rest as the cocktail that defines the City? Does the Martinez fit that profile, or maybe the Pisco punch? Perhaps the most San Francentric cocktail boasts a locally produced spirit paired with farmers' market ingredients? Or is that style just a passing trend? Can a single cocktail exemplify all of the virtues of a city? Might the Sazerac be that cocktail for New Orleans, the gin rickey for Washington, DC, or the Pisco sour for Lima?

If a single drink defines San Francisco, it must hold the history of California in its recipe, and whether shaken or stirred, it must steady a man against a storm while calling forth the sea. It must be light on the palate, yet contain many notes, promises, like an aria written as a letter between lovers. It must be sweet, round, dry, bitter, and salty and call forth grape, grain, agave, and more. Like the people of San Francisco, the drink must be ecumenical and multicultural, innovative yet born of tradition. Is such a cocktail in this book? Perhaps.

In addition to the cocktails, their recipes and lore, you'll find a few essays on the cocktail culture of San Francisco amid the global renaissance of drink and my impassioned endeavors within it, from hosting the world's first cocktail soiree in a farmers' market, conceiving San Francisco Cocktail Week, and teaching a class on San Francisco cocktails to writing this book. If you're like me and hold a sense of passion for a single place—Paris, Poughkeepsie, Portland, or beyond—these pages will resonate with you. And if you love a perfectly prepared, great cocktail and can appreciate it as living history in a chilled glass, this is also the book for you.

Years ago, my wife and I traveled to Istanbul, where our two favorite memories came from visiting the Spice Bazaar and taking a cooking class on traditional Turkish cuisine. Istanbul was, for over a millennia, the crossroads of the world—where Europe met Asia, where Rome once stood and squinted east at the shadow of Genghis Khan. Istanbul, like San Francisco, is a port city, situated on the Bosphorus in the eastern Mediterranean. Its cuisine is a rich tapestry, reflective of its location and influences. Yet every dish we learned to prepare included at least one of three ingredients: lentils, eggplant, or mint. An incredibly rich and storied cuisine in a vibrant and combustible city is rooted in just three foods. That class did the most to illuminate the soul of Istanbul, more than our stroll through the Blue Mosque, more than pausing, resting, whispering during the call to prayer.

When you are in San Francisco, you must step onto the Golden Gate Bridge and experience the sun and the sea, the grand views of little Alcatraz against the City's skyline. But if you're like me, languishing atop a bar stool and soaking in the tales of a San Francisco gone by while sipping on something bright, bitter, and boozy will do more to feed your soul than any stroll ever could.

*Group of unidentified men posing inside the Cuckoos Nest bar, n.d.*

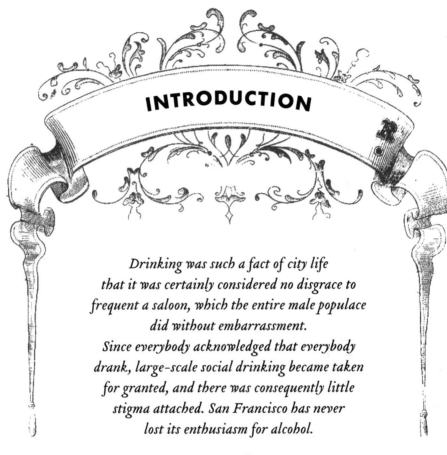

# INTRODUCTION

*Drinking was such a fact of city life
that it was certainly considered no disgrace to
frequent a saloon, which the entire male populace
did without embarrassment.
Since everybody acknowledged that everybody
drank, large-scale social drinking became taken
for granted, and there was consequently little
stigma attached. San Francisco has never
lost its enthusiasm for alcohol.*

—Doris Muscatine, *Old San Francisco*

It's a child's trick to slip a hand into the little jar of cocktail cherries and pluck out a few—a trick I could never resist.

These days, the jar and the cherries are both smaller and my hand much too big. Plus, the cherries are soaked in-house in a mixture of rum and brandy. It's the same reward: thieving, messy, the boozy liquid dribbling back down my fist. Now it's the alcohol, not just the sugar and neon fruit, that beckons, however. I stop and dab my tongue at the thick of my palm just before the beauty runs over my wrist.

I'm standing at the front door of Cantina, looking back into the room, admiring how the shadows cast by the soft Edison bulbs move to flatter her, like a woman *d'un certain âge*. And for a moment I don't want to leave, but I must. If I hurry, I can slip out before the onslaught of humanity floods in for happy hour. If I don't, I'll be stuck: Cantina, Sutter Street, San Francisco, me wearing that quintessential broad smile, opening bottles, regaling my regulars with tall tales, stirring improvised liquid requests, whirling in among the guests, sincerely inquiring about their lives.

Evening triggers the occasion of drink. Folks rush to find a bar stool or booth, then quickly scan the cocktail menu with discerning eyes, so that they might have that first delicious, miraculous sip before the sun sets. It's that inaugural sip, that moment of transition from business to pleasure, that haunts and electrifies: a cold glass in hand with the promise of night coming on. Twilight is a bar's best hour.

I have already tidied up and prepped for service. I don't need to tend bar this evening, which again means that if I am to leave, I must do it now so as not to appear rude. You see, a good bartender knows that if one of his or her better regulars comes in, it isn't just a drink he or she is after. It's also the chat. The chat is part of the commercial exchange, sealed over time by repetition. Good bartenders enjoy the chat, knowing, of course, that it can consume much of their energy over the course of the evening. When an owner is not present, is nowhere to be seen, the barkeeps on duty will relay that fact and do their best to chat up the regulars.

I double-check the work of the prep man and then my own: I have strained and bottled the five-spice agave nectar, fortified the cocktail syrup with nips of rum and sherry, filled in the gaps where bottles were missing on the back bar, and made certain that each cocktail station has the proper set of bar tools. The lighting has been lowered to a gratifying glow, and the volume of every speaker has been carefully balanced and is ready for the night's music. I give the redwood bar top a final wipe, and then, I double-check that one thing that a group of busy bartenders always needs: a stack of clean, dry towels. There, inside the cupboard beneath the beer taps, neatly wedged between the straws and the beverage napkins, is a stack of twenty towels.

\* \* \*

It is a summer's evening in San Francisco, which means that the fog will soon be coming in, cutting off the tops of buildings in its wake. Long ago, when I tended bar in the Starlight Room on the twenty-first floor of the nearby Sir Francis Drake Hotel, it was a pleasure to open the joint at exactly six o'clock to a room of both visitors and locals who would immediately fill the twenty-two stools at the long bar. They would stare out through the bottles lining the back bar, through the windows facing west and watch the fog roll first over Lone Mountain, then across Hayes Valley with only the spire of City Hall visible, and finally blanket all of downtown. The roof of the fog crested near the hotel's eighteenth floor, and so, as I would quickly turn my back to reach for the bottles of spiced rum and curaçao to prepare that signature cocktail, the cable car, I'd look out over a sea of gray with the sun setting in the west and feel as though I'd been transported. There, above the clouds, amid the clinking of little glasses and the hard cracking of ice against tin, all of us felt our lives rise closer to something remarkable.

I cross the cable car tracks on Powell Street and continue east down Sutter, and but a minute later, I hop astride a bar stool inside the Burritt Room. From behind the bar, bottles are flying up spinning in the hands of a most capable barman, their contents of exotic origin releasing shots of grape and cane, sunny pineapple, spiced bitters, and more. Jigger to glass then jigger to mat, then shake, shake, shake. Strained once, twice, and then through the tea strainer, the lovely elixir with its light foam brims to the top of the glass. My East India cocktail is set before me, and in the din, I slowly raise the chilled glass to my lips: that first, momentary, sublime sip. And so, I exhale the day.

I find myself falling into the grasp of the exposed brick walls, the chipped antique tile floor, the sure delight of intoxication prepared by my barkeep. Bottles of homemade bitters and crystal decanters of fresh herbs ready to be spanked, smacked, and muddled line the bar top. The air is alive with citrus that has been recently squeezed and then its peel pinched to release its oils into the martinis below.

The room is thick with couples and cliques of coworkers, laughing and talking a bit too loudly for so early in the evening. Everyone, myself included, feels the unique joy of being here, and as the crowd swells, the din bounces off the brick. Yet no one spills a drink. Cocktails are gripped in the hands of these men and women with almost proprietary care, cradled as if they are precious cargo under paternal watch.

The Burritt Room + Tavern is housed inside the Mystic Hotel on Stockton Street. It's a historic room of sorts, but the business itself is no more than a few years old. An old mahogany bar rises out of the blue-and-blonde tile, separating the thirsty from the bow-tied barmen. The joint is named after a difficult-to-find alley located behind the building. This would seem to be a dull and uninspired fact, unless you were a lover of San Francisco's history, or rather, her fiction: Burritt Alley is where Brigid O'Shaughnessy plugged Miles Archer through the heart in Hammett's noir classic, *The Maltese Falcon*.

A not-so-dull fact is that the Burritt Room sits neatly in the middle of the thickest portion of the San Francisco Cocktail Route, a trail of saloons that took shape in the Gay Nineties and is still alive today. Look at a map of San Francisco and there in Lower Nob Hill, Union Square, and the Financial District, mixologists ply their trade cheek by jowl, the steady soundtrack of shaking, not stirring, fueling the crowded streets.

In spite of my fondness for the Burritt Room, my time to leave comes quickly. I put a crisp Andrew Jackson atop the bar and, like an aging fullback, look for the lanes amid the jostling crowd.

Fortified and with sure feet, I step out from the shelter and the ghost of Sam Spade. Automobiles roar and then whoosh out from the Stockton Tunnel, pushing on into the wind and fog of Union Square, impervious to the night's chill. I dart through the traffic and again head down Sutter Street.

* * *

At Grant Avenue, I turn left and walk beneath the Dragon Gate into Chinatown along what is perhaps the most colorful street in the West. Two of Chinatown's best bars, the Buddha and the Li Po, face each other on the 900 block. The Buddha possesses a vibe of hipster cool on weekends, its down-and-dirty locale making it all the more appealing on a Saturday evening. I opt for the Li Po. A sandwich board leaning precariously against the door proclaims its signature delight: Chinese mai tai. Puzzling etymology, I think; *mai tai* is the Tahitian expression for "the best ever," and further, what could this little hovel have done to improve fellow San Franciscan Trader Vic's tiki masterpiece?

I step inside to find an empty room with an L-shaped bar. Behind the bar, at its apex, stands a large Buddha shrine, with candles and incense glowing, oranges and plastic flowers. B-sides by Michael Jackson reign on the jukebox. I order the Chinese mai tai, and only as the barkeep begins her ritual, do I notice on the back bar a framed certificate of trademark claiming the cocktail's origin. This will be serious, I think. The bartender grabs bottle after bottle—many rums, it seems—and is pouring shot after shot of dark liquor into a blender over ice. I count seven bottles in all, most of them liquor—the rum, a rose-accented sorghum whiskey from China—others not, and of varying colors nature never intended. To confound me, she doesn't blend my mai tai. Instead, she simply pours it from the plastic pitcher into a remnant of a hurricane glass.

The bartender sets the mai tai before me, and as I begin to sip, she stops in front of the Buddha and begins to pray. Bowing several times, she chants in a low voice, pauses, and then resumes her work. Her next task is to open a bottle of Anchor Steam beer for the fellow who has just taken a seat next to me. All the while, Jacko sings.

Strange, in spite of holding nothing fresh, nothing measured, being too strong, and perhaps too sweet, the Li Po's Chinese mai tai is rather pleasing. Trader Vic would be flattered.

* * *

I wander downhill along Washington Street and into Portsmouth Square, and I remember my seventh-grade history: this is where the flag of the United States was first raised in California. Even though it stands in the heart of Chinatown, the square has the feeling of an urban afterthought, an appeasement against the skyscrapers plumb along its border. I remind myself that this little piece of land is where civilization, culture, and, especially, cocktails began in the West. Banks and saloons—and gold—all came to what was San Francisco's first town square. There, across Kearny Street, the City Hall of San Francisco once stood, and next to it, the El Dorado, where a young Jerry Thomas learned his trade—the trade that made him America's first famous mixologist.

San Francisco, since that discovery of gold in the spring of 1848, has become a collection of global intersections and celebratory explosions. And, having just penned that, it occurs to me that the same could be writ of her cocktails: a delicious collection brought together by global intersection for the occasion of explosive celebration! Jerry Thomas's signature whiskey cocktail the blue blazer was stirred, set afire, and then dramatically poured in a flaming arc through the night air for a pretty penny, or a little gold. Gold nuggets then and gold cards now are slammed atop the bar. Liquid delights have flowed into the Port of San Francisco through the hands of capable mixologists and out from coupes and flutes and into our mouths since gold brought them and all of us here.

It wasn't just the nouveau riche who drank in the public palaces that lined Montgomery Street. Prospectors would return to civilization after months of panning for gold in the Sierras, their pockets empty, their bodies tired, their souls parched. Here, the other, infamous side of the Barbary Coast existed to serve these down-and-out dreamers and to supply them with quick drink, even if it was their last. This created a dichotomy in the character of San Francisco, a dichotomy that still defines it today: San Francisco is a stunningly beautiful city of great taste in which all of the debauchery of the world can be found. It was 160 years ago—before San Francisco gave rise to jazz, before she played host to the sexual revolution, that prospector and political progressive Hinton Helper penned, "I have seen purer liquors, better segars, finer tobacco, truer guns and pistols, larger dirks and bowie knives, and prettier courtesans here in San Francisco than in any other place I have ever visited; and it is my unbiased opinion that California can and does furnish the best bad things that are available in America."

* * *

*Nightclubs on Pacific Street in the Barbary Coast District, 1909*

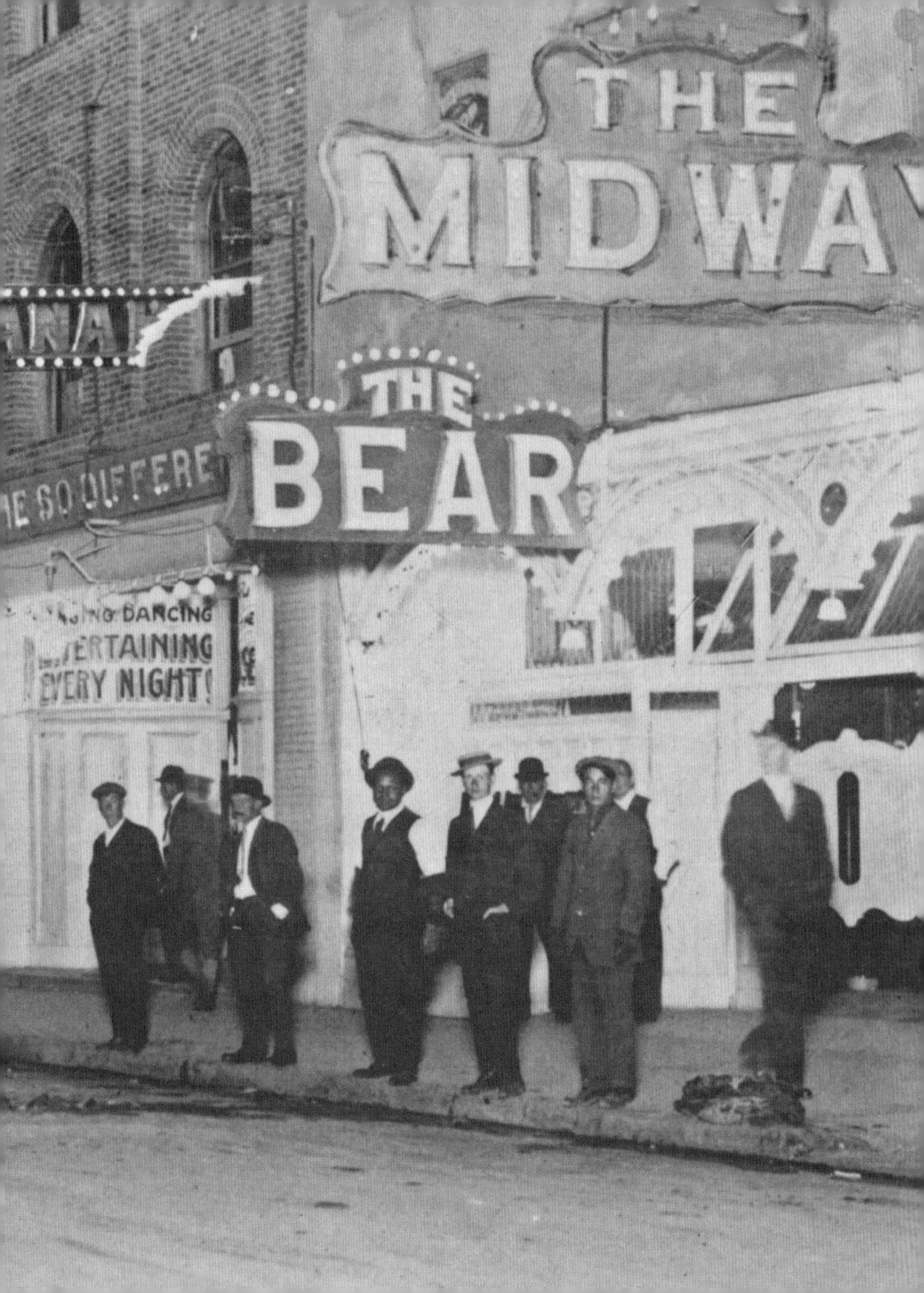
THE
MIDWA
THE
BEAR
DANCING
EVERY NIGHT!

*Montgomery Avenue (now Columbus Avenue) looking west, 1890*

COMMERCIAL HOTEL
RESTAURANT

LAW
OFFICE

LAW
OFFICE

T.E. HECHT
430-35TH AVE.

# NO. 1

## THE MARTINEZ

*Created by Jerry Thomas, championed in its later form by*
*Winston Churchill, and swilled by millions*

## MARTINEZ

1½ oz/45 ml No. 209 gin

¾ oz/20 ml Vya sweet (Italian) vermouth

¼ oz/10 ml maraschino liqueur

2 dashes orange bitters

Expressed lemon peel for garnish

Pour the liquid into a mixing glass, add ice, stir forty times, then
strain into a cocktail coupe, garnish with the lemon peel, and
serve with a smile.

The Martinez, delicious, bracing, round, and brimming with booze, is a creation of superior beauty. God didn't make it; man did. And now, at the Comstock Saloon, where Terrific Street crosses Columbus Avenue, a beautiful lass stands behind the wood ready to stir San Francisco's most important export.

The cocktail that has come to define cocktails tastes and looks nothing like the one Professor Jerry Thomas slung on a foggy afternoon in San Francisco some 150 years ago and dubbed the Martinez. A San Francisco original, the martini came to be called just that no later than 1882, when Harry Johnson listed it—or at least an astoundingly similar cocktail called, yes, the martini—in his *New and Improved Bartender's Manual*. Nine years later, the third member of the Barbary Coast's nineteenth-century barmen-as-authors tribe, "Cocktail Bill" Boothby, included the martini cocktail in his *Cocktail Boothby's American Bar-Tender*. By the turn of the twentieth century, the efforts of these three Barbary Coast barmen had made the martini a global cocktail.

There are theories aplenty on which bartender actually created the drink and on whether the name was changed because the drink called for Martini & Rossi vermouth from Italy or because, as often happens, it (and its recipe) was simply altered over the course of decades, the details now forgotten. (To muddy the tale even further, across San Pablo Bay, in the little town of Martinez, a sign in an abandoned lot claims that, in 1849, the Martinez was created on that very patch of land.) None of that matters to the passionate San Franciscan, however, for whom the paternity of the martini is certain.

By the era of Winston Churchill, he and his famed passion and palate for plenty of gin made it fashionable simply to wave the bottle of vermouth—now both dry and French—over the cocktail glass, making the martini cocktail just gin, very cold, in a glass.

A martini came to symbolize luxury and escape, and, much later, it evolved into anything served in a stemmed glass. Ian Fleming, the spy novelist who penned the James Bond books, was obsessed with the Cold War and with what lay on the other side of the Iron Curtain: Vodka. At the time, vodka produced by Mother Russia and its communist ethos was forbidden. The fictional Bond, like the real Sir Francis Drake centuries earlier (see page 129), liked to drink of his enemy's nectar. Vodka was exotic and strong, and so, because of the Bond films, the martini came chiefly to be made with vodka—shaken, not stirred. Then, the same cocktail took on liqueurs, fruits, and other various flavorings du jour.

The martini experienced a long, steady growth until the mid-twentieth century, when those various iterations became unstoppable. The story of the Martinez, however, is a story of resilience, of survival. If we were to study its DNA, we would see how well it has always adapted to its surroundings. Indeed, in the world of cocktails, it is the best success story. But it is also one of the strangest. It started out vermouth based, slung with

*Kearny Street north of Pacific Avenue, San Francisco, 1892*

KEARNY ST N FROM PACIF

(perhaps inferior) Old Tom gin and sweetened with either maraschino liqueur or gum syrup. It then morphed into a straight vodka drink (with blue cheese olives, anyone?). Over the course of a century, millions of martinis, all of them shaken and bruised, were imbibed. Then, suddenly, the Martinez returns, resurrected and stirred slowly. It shows up on cocktail menus throughout the City, across the lower forty-eight, and in London and Melbourne. The Martinez has come full circle and is once again tied to its origin.

Today, if you were to sit astride a bar stool in the Comstock Saloon and open the cocktail menu, you would see a Martinez that is remarkably similar to the drink that Jerry Thomas pushed across the pine at the Occidental Hotel, just a few blocks away. And through the Comstock's floor-to-ceiling windows you would have a view of that little triangle of land known as Devil's Acre; at its apex stands a café, also with floor-to-ceiling windows, that specializes in single-pour coffees and caters to young adults in Levi's and cream-colored coats who sit quietly immersed in their laptops. For a moment, the Devil's Acre looks as though it is scrubbed clean. Then, from the barkeep's iPod, Johnny Cash begins to howl and that bright, slightly bitter, and altogether boozy Martinez still sits expectantly atop the bar. The lass behind the wood laughs as she shakes two cocktails simultaneously, and you're right back where you want to be.

## Marguerite
*By Harry Johnson*

1½ oz/45 ml gin

1½ oz/45 ml dry vermouth

3 dashes absinthe

3 dashes orange bitters

Expressed lemon peel for garnish

Pour the liquid into a mixing glass, add ice, stir forty times, then strain into a cocktail coupe and garnish with the lemon peel and serve.

## Gill Sans
*By Jeff Hollinger, courtesy of Comstock Saloon*

Absinthe for rinsing glass

2 oz/60 ml gin

¾ oz/20 ml manzanilla sherry

¼ oz/10 ml maraschino liqueur

2 dashes orange bitters

Expressed lemon peel for garnish

Pour a small amount of absinthe into a cocktail coupe, swirl the glass to cover the inside with liquid, and pour out the excess. Pour the gin, sherry, maraschino liqueur, and bitters into a mixing glass, add ice, stir forty times, then strain into the absinthe-rinsed cocktail coupe and garnish with the lemon peel.

## Laura Palmer
*By Charlie Russo, courtesy of Blackbird*

1¾ oz/50 ml gin

1 oz/30 ml Lillet Blanc

¼ oz/10 ml Bénédictine D.O.M.

Brandied cherry and juice for garnish

Pour the liquid into a mixing glass, add ice, stir forty times, then strain into a cocktail coupe and garnish with the cherry and a little splash of the cherry juice.

# ON GIN

My experience with gin is similar to that of many barkeeps: I came to it late and then fell violently in love. Growing up, gin held associations of yesteryear, childhood memories of holidays at my grandparents' house. Then came teenage and college fêtes a few hundred strong, followed by the stink of kitchen tile the morning after—dying citrus stuck to the floor, bright alcohol, sticky sweet tonic—experiences that clung to my psyche until I was well into my thirties. (Clearly, much gin had been consumed in all the wrong ways.) Only then did I realize gin's merits, its great history, and its greater contribution to cocktails.

A few years ago, with my mind cocktail focused, I worked on creating the flavor and formulation for Bombay Sapphire East, selecting a new botanical blend and a lowered level of alcohol. Why? Because sometimes a little change can make a big difference: great gins perform wonders in the tin (the barkeep's Boston shaker), giving new life to cocktails such as the Negroni and the last word. That's what the best gin can and should do: make old drinks perfect for today.

From time to time, I meander down to Pier 50 along San Francisco's south waterfront to Distillery No. 209, where I find Arne Hillesland hard at work distilling his No. 209 gin. There, above the scent of salt water from the bay, I find Arne dwarfed beneath the five-thousand-liter Scottish alembic still he cooks on, cloaked in the aroma of bergamot and clove, juniper and cardamom.

"Distilling gin in San Francisco is such a perfect match," Arne tells me. "Gin has long been associated with seafaring, and here I am, the luckiest guy in the world, making gin in the world's only distillery built over water. Also, gin is favored by drinkers with discerning palates, and San Francisco is one of the best foodie cities in the world. Plus, the unique smorgasbord of flavors that are incorporated into gin make it a delight in a well-made cocktail!"

Arne the Distiller is built like a butcher: barrel-chested with the thickest of forearms. But his demeanor is never gruff, and as he speaks, he pauses to sniff lightly and is gone for a moment. "Do you smell that?" he asks me.

"What should I be smelling?" I reply, sensing a trick question.

"The botanicals simmer together in the alcohol, but each has a different way of reacting to the alcohol and heat, each does so at separate times, and the aromas and essential oils float out into the ether. . . ."

"Coriander!" I offer.

"Yes!" comes his affirmation. But I look at him and see that it's too late. I've lost him. The Ginerator, as he prefers to be called, is in his element.

I walk outside the little distillery into the open air along the dock. I stare out at giant cargo vessels carrying the world's goods in and out of the Port of Oakland. Behind me, the Ginerator grabs a bottle of No. 209 gin, a bottle of tonic, glasses, and goes about fixing a pair of cocktails—he and I both prefer our drinks with lemon—and then joins me outdoors and hands me a drink. "Thank you," I say, as I lean against the railing, listening to the sloshing of the little waves below, the anxious cry of seagulls all about. Then, from the near distance, comes the din of forty thousand baseball fans at AT&T Park cheering on the San Francisco Giants at an afternoon game. After a sip, Arne continues where he had left off.

"The closest way I can think to describe the distilling of gin is like a jazz combo. At any one point, someone in the combo is playing a solo while all the others are supporting, each instrument waiting, lingering in the background. Then, that soloist fades and a new soloist comes front and center. The same process happens with our botanicals during distillation. No. 209 gin does not fully come into being until the song, or the distillation batch, is finally finished. Magic, I say."

# THE BARTENDER'S SECRET FORMULA

Blending spirits in-house may, at first, sound apocryphal: taking bits from some bottles and employing them in others, evolving the nature of the base spirit as you go. However, it isn't at all apocryphal. It is instead wholly natural and, perhaps, the way of the future.

The first few cocktail books ever published were written for the trade: bartenders and the saloon keepers who employed them. The audience was male, and the writing was sparse, pragmatic, and geared toward helping the saloon keeper save a buck. Some of these books, such as "Cocktail Bill" Boothby's *Cocktail Boothby's American Bar-Tender*, provided recipes on how to re-create certain spirits and to fake popular brands and products for when the saloon was out of stock or, frankly, didn't care to spend the money. The exercise was to combine disparate elements to match the look and taste of gin, Cognac, whiskey, and so on, all for cheap.

These recipes never thought to emphasize appellation or a sense of respect for the history of the liquids they chose to mimic. The assumption was that the drinking public wouldn't know the difference.

Today, we live in a world in which an average drinker sitting at an average bar has, in fact, visited multiple distilleries, spent several weekends at winery cottages, and whiled away many an afternoon at a local brewery. In short, the intellectual property has never been higher, and the palates of cocktail drinkers never more discerning.

The same is true for the men and women working behind-the-stick. The reason that cocktails have never tasted better, have never been more interesting, even astounding in their balanced freshness, is because of the crop of educated talent tending bar in San Francisco and across the land. Bartenders are the individuals best able to make decisions concerning which rye whiskey works best in a Manhattan and which bourbon is ideally suited for a mint julep. Unfortunately, the producers of spirits don't always understand the means by which their bottles get emptied—cocktails, anyone?—and so most brands in any spirit category have a limited bandwidth. (I'm not advocating that every brand that enters the marketplace hold liquid built entirely with a cocktail strategy in mind; nor am I dismissing the notion entirely.) Enter the bartender who has become a mixologist and has many opinions on the spirits he or she uses the most.

Which gin do you prefer in your aviation, your Negroni, or your French 75? Or which whiskey do you like in your Manhattan, your old fashioned, or your whiskey sour? If the answer is a different brand in each one, the time has come for you to blend your own spirits. All of my recipes for spirits in this book are based

THE REASON THAT COCKTAILS HAVE NEVER TASTED BETTER, HAVE NEVER BEEN MORE INTERESTING, EVEN ASTOUNDING IN THEIR BALANCED FRESH-NESS, IS BECAUSE OF THE CROP OF EDUCATED TALENT TENDING BAR IN SAN FRANCISCO AND ACROSS THE LAND. BARTENDERS ARE THE INDIVIDU-ALS BEST ABLE TO MAKE DECISIONS CONCERNING WHICH RYE WHISKEY WORKS BEST IN A MANHATTAN AND WHICH BOURBON IS IDEALLY SUITED FOR A MINT JULEP.

on economical performance: First, what can you—the individual or the bar—afford? And second, what gin, whiskey, or other spirit performs best in a slew of popular cocktails, especially the recipes in these pages? This exercise presents an opportunity for you to become a Master Blender!

The instructions for creating your own blended spirit are fairly simple. Always approach different gins, whiskeys, or whatever spirit you are blending as separate lots (barrels, tanks), if you will. Each has its own unique merit, and the complete blend will rely on utilizing

the characteristics of each to deliver a symphony of flavor. Begin by blending the distillates and any other ingredients into a large vessel, such as a 1-gal/3.8-L pitcher, or even a 6-gal/22.7-L Cambro bucket with a faucet dispenser. Follow the instructions in each formula for how long the blended spirit should rest before using.

*Spider Kelly's Bar Room, San Francisco, 1911*

# SUPERIOR COCKTAIL OLD TOM GIN

My reasons for blending cocktail Old Tom gin the way I do here are straightforward: Beefeater produces a classic and affordable London dry gin. When blended with the hearty and highly spiced No. 209 gin, it gains strength.

Add a nip of Plymouth gin for robust mouthfeel and a dollop of amontillado sherry and suddenly that tannic strength with a slight edge is brightened and ever so slightly lengthened.

Splash in the slightest bit of cocktail syrup, and this gin tastes as only an improved Old Tom gin can and should. It absolutely sings in cocktails and elevates such classics as the French 75, the gin fizz, and, especially, the Martinez.

**Bartender's Secret Formula: Superior Cocktail Old Tom Gin**

20 oz/600 ml Beefeater London dry gin

7 oz/200 ml No. 209 gin

3½ oz/100 ml Plymouth gin

1¾ oz/50 ml amontillado sherry

1¾ oz/50 ml Cocktail Syrup (page 59)

Blend the liquid into a large vessel, such as a 1-gal/3.8-L pitcher, then allow to rest for 1 week before using.

*Makes 1 qt/1 L*

*Bank Exchange, SE corner Montgomery and Washington Streets, n.d.*

# ON VERMOUTH

Vermouth, wine that has been oxidized, aromatized, sweetened, and then fortified, is one of mankind's oldest beverages, predating distillation of alcohol by at least a thousand years ago. In those early days, herbs and honey masked the taste of the oxidized wine. When it was discovered that mixing eau-de-vie into wine fortified it for long keeping, wine making was changed forever, and vermouth—the word comes from the German *Vermut*, for "wormwood"—was born.

On the Barbary Coast in the nineteenth century, bartenders didn't have the choice of dry or sweet vermouth in their cocktails, as only sweet vermouth was available. (Dry, or French, vermouth was not imported into the United States until the early twentieth century.) The brands were predominantly from Italy, and the bottles were labeled simply vermouth, with no nod to the sweetness of their contents. Italian vermouth was a staple of San Francisco mixology in those years, perhaps more so than any other ingredient, and the great cocktails and punches of the era, especially the Martinez, owed their existence to it.

Looking back, that popularity is surprising, given that most people don't like the bitter flavor of wormwood, the classic component of vermouth. Interestingly,

vermouth made in countries that are members of the European Union (EU) must include wormwood in its formula, even if it is only a tiny fraction of a percent. In the United States, no such requirement exists. Here, and particularly in California, we follow the spirit of the old law: vermouth should taste and act like vermouth whether or not it has wormwood in it. Neither of the two vermouth brands produced in California, Sutton Cellars and Vya, contains wormwood.

In the southeast lane of San Francisco, in the burgeoning district of Dogpatch, you'll find a winery inside what appears to be a storage facility—or what could pass as a parking garage. That winery is Sutton Cellars, which specializes in producing fortified, aromatized wines, specifically vermouth. No sign announces it, its fabled image appears nowhere on an exterior wall, and no vines are growing nearby. A loud knock on an anonymous door is what it takes to get in, and then a wily hoot owl of a man, a winemaker with a substantial mustache who has ingested more alcohol and herbs than anyone I know, boldly swings the door his way: Carl Sutton has opened the door, and you are now inside his kingdom.

Sutton Cellars, a single, long concrete room, is the home of the vermouth renaissance in America. Vermouth, Carl tells me, is "the perfect intermezzo. It provides the transition in the day between being social at work and being social at play. Vermouth as an aperitif marks a specific time and place during one's day." I couldn't agree more. I love a delicious aperitif, a light, bright something to change my day into night. But for the readers of this book, cocktail lovers, I asked Carl what specific drink he recommends to begin the evening?

"A Sutton and soda," he replies. That is, in fact, his signature cocktail, and for half a decade, it has been a staple in many restaurants and craft cocktail bars across the City.

"I have yet to see enough vermouth in cocktails," Carl says. Interesting perspective, I think to myself, and a strong sentiment from a man who has made a living selling handmade, hand-bottled vermouth out of a garage to restaurants across San Francisco. "But vermouth is ubiquitous," I counter. "And Sutton Cellars is distinctive within vermouth."

"True," he says, in between breaths of blowing his mustache and then refilling our glasses with something from one of his many barrels. "It's true. San Francisco consumers do have an open mind. They understand and are not afraid of vermouth being a unique type of fortified wine, to be enjoyed and consumed within a few weeks of every bottle's opening."

On that subject, Carl and I are in complete agreement. For as much prescriptive bickering as there has been in the last decade on throwing out old vermouth or storing your vermouth in the refrigerator, two things are certain: Industrial vermouth is intentionally shelf-stable via oxidation, fortification, and sweetening with caramel—it is meant to last. And second, any bar or cocktail enthusiast who understands his or her drinks will realize that a 750-milliliter bottle of single-barrel Sutton Cellars vermouth holds enough liquid to slowly stir thirty-three Manhattans or Martinezes, twenty-five Negronis, or eight Sutton and sodas. I asked Jeff Hollinger, proprietor of the Comstock Saloon and coauthor of The Art of the Bar, how long a single bottle of vermouth resides in the speed rail of Comstock before being depleted? "Are you joking?" he retorted. "We make classic cocktails here. A bottle a shift, at minimum."

I appreciate Hollinger's enthusiasm. You see, a great cocktail bar understands its cocktail ingredients, and inherent in that is a commitment to the good, the fresh, the unique. Therein is the unique something-so-special about a great bar, about great cocktails, where vermouth is consumed in quantity.

# SUPERIOR COCKTAIL VERMOUTH

Vermouth grew out the ancient practice of preserving and flavoring wine. Now, of course, it is an intentionally oxidized, aromatized, fortified, and sweetened wine, highly mixable, and it can be crafted from a variety of fortified grape sources, as long as the end result is the same. For example, in the popular *vermuterias* of Spain, which are becoming the hip watering holes of choice among the country's youth, bartenders make their own vermouth by purchasing barrels of wine and brandy and then blending and flavoring the vermouth in-house.

Here is my recipe for a vermouth cocktail blend, which is an improvement on the classic Italian, or sweet, vermouth because it carries a broader mouthfeel and more complex herbal notes. Before the advent of wine making on an industrial scale in the twentieth century, sweet vermouth was produced from red wine grapes and dry vermouth was produced from white wine grapes. Not so today. Most of the world's sweet vermouth is produced with white wine, then colored with caramel. The rich notes that only red fruit can deliver are missing, of course—the same notes that originally worked so beautifully in the Martinez, the Manhattan, and other early cocktails.

Based on nimble Pinot Noir, my vermouth cocktail blend includes Madeira made from the common Tinta Negra Mole varietal, prized for its rich, ripe grapey flavor.

The amaro brings both a bitter spice with supple notes of chocolate and increased alcohol to fortify the vermouth. Cream sherry adds a viscous sweetness, while the *bianco* (white) vermouth adds light vanilla and bright citrus. This blended spirit is imminently mixable, of course, as in the Boothby Cocktail (a Manhattan variation) on page 102, but is also plenty delicious on its own, over ice, and with seltzer.

Question: To refrigerate or not to refrigerate vermouth to keep it fresh for cocktails?

Answer: Use more vermouth, to make more cocktails with more frequency!

## The Bartender's Secret Formula: Superior Cocktail Vermouth

20 oz/600 ml Pinot Noir

7 oz/200 ml amaro, such as Averna or Nonino

3½ oz/100 ml bianco (sweet white) vermouth, such as Cinzano or Dolin

1¾ oz/50 ml cream sherry

1¾ oz/50 ml aged Madeira, made from the Tinta Negra Mole grape

Blend the liquid into a large vessel, such as a 1-gal/3.8-L pitcher, then allow to rest for 1 week before using.

*Makes 1 qt/1 L*

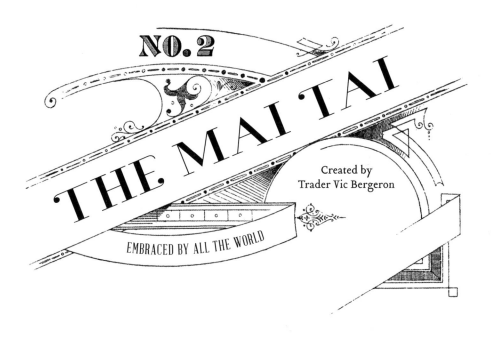

# NO. 2

## THE MAI TAI

Created by
Trader Vic Bergeron

*EMBRACED BY ALL THE WORLD*

## MAI TAI

2 oz/60 ml Sergeant Classick gold rum

¾ oz/20 ml fresh lime juice, with ½ spent lime
reserved for garnish

½ oz/15 ml almond syrup

¼ oz/10 ml orange curaçao

¼ oz/10 ml Cocktail Syrup (page 59)

Pour the liquid into a mixing glass, fill with crushed ice, shake
vigorously for a second, and pour all into a rocks glass. Garnish
with the spent lime hull, relax, and enjoy.

Tracking down a perfect, classic mai tai—one that contains neither pineapple juice nor anything to impart a pink tint—happens only rarely nowadays. Although the cocktail's paternity has been argued, its crisp simplicity is not up for debate, especially in San Francisco, where Trader Vic Bergeron was born and raised and saw his career flourish.

Like many others, I've vacationed in Hawaii, the seeming spiritual home of the mai tai. And there, in the hotels along Waikiki or on the beaches of Maui, I've sucked back many mai tais. I have even enjoyed completely different recipes for the mai tai in the same bar, because in Hawaii, it seems as if every bartender has his or her own mai tai recipe. I've swilled mai tais made with white rum, aged rum, dark rum, and spiced rum, and with lime juice, pineapple juice, orange juice, Triple Sec, and many flavored sugar syrups. They have come doused with amaretto, grenadine, and even the much maligned blue curaçao. So, which one is the real mai tai?

A perfect, classic mai tai can be had from the hands of tiki savant Martin Cate, the proprietor of Smuggler's Cove in San Francisco and an old bar dog who learned his trade behind-the-stick at a Trader Vic's restaurant. A mai tai made by Martin isn't the bastardized cruise-ship phenom that arrives oversize, pink, sweet, and frothy. A mai tai from Martin is the crisp Trader Vic's original that has been replicated across San Francisco.

On the palate, Martin's mai tai most closely resembles a nutty rum margarita: dry, round, bright, and citric. When made well, a mai tai can actually be paired with many foods. Flavor is what inspired Vic Bergeron when he invented this cocktail, and the many dishes of his namesake Polynesian restaurants. The Bergeron family was of French ancestry, and Vic's orgeat syrup was a homemade recipe, a potent flavor from his childhood. Orgeat first became a component in San Francisco mixology with the arrival of some thirty thousand French citizens in the early 1850s, who brought with them their culinary products and preferences. It was an ingredient that held a singular sense of place and would later inform many of Vic's cocktails. Vic married that uniquely ethnic ingredient from France and the San Francisco tradition of mixology to create what many believe is the most Polynesian cocktail of all time. Yes, only in San Francisco. . . .

# MAKE YOUR OWN ORGEAT SYRUP

This recipe is courtesy of Daniel Shoemaker, an expat San Franciscan and proprietor of Teardrop Lounge in Portland, Oregon. Daniel and I spent a few years tending bar together in San Francisco more than a decade ago.

2¼ cups/530 g sliced raw almonds

7 cups/1.7 L distilled water

½ cup/100 g organic cane sugar

2 Tbsp/30 ml silver rum

¼ tsp orange flower water

Put the almonds in a bowl, add half of the water, and let sit for 30 minutes. Drain the almonds, discarding the water. Transfer the almonds to a food processor and pulse just until coarsely ground. Return the almonds to the bowl, add the remaining water, and let the mixture sit at room temperature for 4 to 5 hours, stirring once every hour.

Line a fine-mesh sieve with cheesecloth and place it over a 1-qt/1-L jar. Strain the almond mixture through the sieve into the jar, then press on the almonds with the back of a spoon to extract as much liquid as possible. (Discard the almond pulp, or save for another use.) Add the sugar to the jar, cap the jar tightly, and shake vigorously until the sugar is completely dissolved. Uncover, add the rum and orange flower water, and stir to incorporate. Re-cover and store in the refrigerator for 2 weeks before using. It will keep for up to 3 months.

*Makes about 1 qt/1 L*

## Fogcutter

*By Trader Vic Bergeron*

1½ oz/45 ml pot-distilled rum, such as
Mount Gay or Plantation

1 oz/30 ml Pisco, such as Campo
de Encanto Dist. RSV Single Vine
Quebranta

1 oz/30 ml fresh lime juice

½ oz/15 ml fresh orange juice

½ oz/15 ml London dry gin

½ oz/15 ml cream sherry

½ oz/15 ml orgeat syrup, homemade
(see page 55) or store-bought

Orange wheel for garnish

Pour the liquid into a mixing glass, add
ice, shake vigorously, and strain into a
giant punch glass filled with cracked ice.
Garnish with the orange wheel.

## Dead Reckoning

*By Martin Cate*

2 oz/60 ml aged rum, such as
Appleton Estate Reserve or El Dorado
5 Year

½ oz/15 ml House-Made Vanilla-
Cognac Cordial (facing page)

½ oz/15 ml grade A maple syrup

½ oz/15 ml tawny port

1 oz/30 ml fresh lemon juice

1 oz/30 ml pineapple juice

Dash Homemade Aromatic Bitters
(page 104)

Fresh mint sprig for garnish

Lemon twist for garnish

Pour the liquid into a mixing glass, add
ice, shake vigorously, and strain into a tall
glass filled with cracked ice. Garnish with
the mint sprig and lemon twist.

## Wilson's Smash

*By Brandon Josie, courtesy of
15 Romolo*

5 to 10 fresh mint leaves, plus 1 sprig
for garnish

2 oz/60 ml aged rum, such as
Bacardi 8 or Ron Zacapa

1 oz/30 ml fresh lime juice

¾ oz/20 ml pineapple cordial,
homemade (see page 70) or
store-bought

2 dashes Homemade Aromatic Bitters
(page 104)

Dash absinthe

Lightly muddle the mint leaves in a mixing
glass, then pour in the liquid and shake.
Strain into a tall glass filled with ice and
garnish with the mint sprig.

## House-Made Vanilla-Cognac Cordial

*Add three vanilla beans to one 750-ml
bottle of Cognac and leave to infuse
for 2 weeks. Strain through a fine-mesh
sieve into a large bowl, and discard the
vanilla beans (or save them for flavoring
a canister of sugar). Add ½ cup/120 ml
Cocktail Syrup (page 59) and mix well.
Transfer to one or more bottles, cap
tightly, and store in the refrigerator for
up to 6 months.
Makes a scant 5 cups/1.1 L*

On the Making of

# PROPER COCKTAIL SYRUP

Simple syrup has never been just that. Sugar and water work wonders in different proportions, and when a syrup is made correctly, it turns cocktails into magical potions.

A decade ago, when I was tending bar at frisson, San Francisco's restaurant du jour, I was experimenting with different recipes for simple syrup (a.k.a. cocktail syrup) one afternoon, and the pastry chef walked in from the prep kitchen. I shared with him that I was blending various types of sugar for the house syrup, that I no longer wanted the blend boiled but merely warmed, and that I'd be salting it as well. The chef, who was (and likely still is) older than me, laughed loudly my way.

"What's so funny?" I asked.

"You're cooking sugar and water. It's not that complicated."

"You use different types of sugar in your pastries, don't you?"

"Yes."

"And you experiment with different temperatures to get the best results, right?"

"Yes. Yes, I do. Fine!" he stammered. "But salting sugar and water is just plain stupid.

It's salty-sweet water!" he exclaimed, then threw the soufflé dish in his right hand to the floor, sending ceramic shards careening across the tile.

I did not sweep up the broken dish, but I did proceed to remove the pot from the stove, allow the mix to cool, bottle my syrup, and then employ it in a thousand cocktails—salt and all.

You see, the taste and texture of white, brown, and turbinado sugars are different from one another and unique. Playing with the Brix level (the measurable amount of sugar in the liquid)—in other words, experimenting with different ratios of sugar to water to see whether you prefer a one-to-one ratio or something higher—and with different types of sugar is how you find out what you like. And whatever conclusion you come to, your cocktail syrup will create a different flavor from another cocktail syrup that uses a different Brix level and mix of sugars.

Over time, I found that I also wanted to further brighten every cocktail that demands a bit of sugar. How would I do that? If cocktail syrup is the consistent ingredient connecting a Sazerac to a daiquiri to a Pisco punch to a mojito, then adjusting that syrup would be the answer.

I began to peel lemons and oranges, express the peels over the top of the syrup, and then drop in the handful of peels. The peels would then steep in the salty-sweet liquid as I gently stirred.

My blend of multiple sugar sources was now tasting great—a vibrant mix of different textures, both bright and rich. And because the way we all typically enhance the flavor of our food—that is, the way we turn up the volume toward our palates—is by using salt, it seemed like the perfect addition. It creates a richer depth of flavor that delivers more information on the tongue, imparting a delicious memory. That means that a little salt is a must for all syrups.

Finally, I insist on fortifying my cocktail syrup for two reasons: it keeps the syrup stable (unfermented) for a longer period of time and it adds more mouthfeel and layers of flavor. Today, I add both silver rum and cream sherry to my cocktail syrup, and the result is absolutely delightful.

Baking—like the bringing together of sugar, salt, and water—is a science, one bent on the necessity of time, of chemistry, of composition and balance. I hope that my old colleague has since seen the error of his ways, or that he has at least forgiven me for somehow stepping on what seemed like his last good nerve.

## Cocktail Syrup

9 cups/2.1 L water

7 cups/1.4 kg granulated sugar

1 cup/220 g firmly packed light or dark brown sugar

1 cup/220 g turbinado sugar

Peel of 2 lemons

Peel of 1 orange

2 tsp salt

½ cup/120 ml silver rum

¼ cup/60 ml cream sherry

In a large saucepan, heat the water over medium heat to just under a boil. Add the three sugars and stir to mix well. Turn the heat to low, add the citrus peels and salt, and stir just until the sugars are fully dissolved. Remove from the heat and let steep for 1 hour.

Strain through a fine-mesh sieve into a large bowl and discard the citrus peels. Add the rum and sherry and stir to mix thoroughly. Transfer to bottles, cap tightly, and store in the refrigerator for up to 3 months.

*Makes about 4 qt/4 L*

# DISTILLED SUGARCANE

The exterior of Smuggler's Cove is less than inviting. The modern facade of glass and steel betrays nothing of what you find inside. "All the more reason to wow our guests when they arrive," explains Martin Cate. And when you do step into Smuggler's Cove for the first time, the experience is jaw-dropping. The interior is so bold, so transporting, that it has moved patrons to fits of giggles. Smuggler's Cove displays the essence of tiki in the place tiki once took shape and commanded an era. "Tiki, or Polynesian pop," Martin says, "is an idealized midcentury version of Polynesian culture, an absolute artifice without authenticity." Smuggler's Cove is an exquisite arrangement of the best of tiki, complete with fixtures that once decorated the original Trader Vic's restaurant.

But this quintessential San Francisco institution is more than just a place to marvel at the lively mix of tiki and nautical decor. It also offers a painstakingly curated cocktail program and is the academic hub of rum on the West Coast.

When you step up to the bar, you are given a cocktail menu that lists more than seventy drinks, many of them calling for upward of eight, even eleven different ingredients in each. Then, behind the little bar, are shelves lined with hundreds of the most exquisite rums the world has to offer. Here, you can receive the greatest education on cane distillates available by joining Martin Cate's Rumbustion Society.

As a fellow barman, I was offered membership in the society, though I politely declined. (My education comes from having visited rum distilleries in Latin America, wielded a machete to harvest sugarcane, and tasted dark, syrupy molasses as it ferments.) What the Rumbustion Society teaches is organoleptic evaluation, or how to taste, as well as the storied history of this beloved spirit in a glass.

Rum, which is the distilled by-product of fermented sugarcane juice, or molasses, can be made anywhere in the world, but its production is concentrated in the Caribbean and in Central and South America. Although it is not the first spirit of the Americas, it is connected to the movements of its people more than any other spirit, and its history cannot be separated from its politics, from the shame of the old slave trade and the leveraging of economies in developing countries. Rum is the spirit of the Everyman, and it just may be the distillate from which more cocktails have been invented than any other. Whether bottled as silver (white), spiced, blackstrap, or a hearty *añejo*, rum is a reflection of its origin. Rum from Jamaica is different than rum from Barbados, which is different than rum from Cuba or Guyana or from one of the artisanal distilleries producing it here in California. There are books of hundreds of pages each that describe these appellations in great detail, of course. But then there is the Rumbustion Society at Smuggler's Cove, San Francisco, with all of the rums you can ever imagine right there for you to enjoy.

*Interior of Trader Vic's Restaurant, n.d.*

# NO. 3

## THE PISCO PUNCH

*Quaffed mightily by Mark Twain and Tom Sawyer;*
*perfected by Duncan Nicol in the Gay Nineties*

### PISCO PUNCH

2 oz/60 ml Campo de Encanto Grand & Noble Pisco

1 oz/30 ml pineapple cordial,
homemade (see page 70) or store-bought

1 oz/30 fresh lime juice

½ oz/15 ml Lillet Rouge or your favorite red wine

Dash aromatic bitters,
homemade (see page 104) or store-bought

Expressed orange peel for garnish

Pour the liquid into a mixing glass, add ice,
shake vigorously, then fine-strain into a cocktail goblet.
Garnish with the orange peel.

People walking along Montgomery Street subconsciously quicken their steps. Montgomery is a four-lane highway, often in gridlock, bordered by the tallest buildings in the City. It cuts through the financial center, a fact that was established as early as 1853 with the opening of the Bank Exchange Building.

I'm standing where the Montgomery Block once stood, near the corner of Washington, and hundreds of citizens are passing me on this early morning, rushing off to their careers. I doubt if any of them know the old stories of this place, of what was once here, where the Transamerica Pyramid now soars far into the sky. I feel a touch of melancholy, as though everyone who rushes through these ghosts should know they've crossed sacred ground.

At this very corner, inside the legendary Montgomery Block, the brightest star that ever shone on a particular bar and its signature delight beamed on the Bank Exchange Saloon and its Pisco punch. Perhaps you've heard, as I have, that old saying, reading it here and there in books, "A visitor to San Francisco must absolutely do three things: ride a cable car, watch the sun set through the Golden Gate, and drink a Pisco punch!" No one knows who originated the saying, but it is known that the saloon and its famous tipple captured the attention of an era.

The Bank Exchange Saloon is held aloft as the Hope Diamond of drinkers' palaces, lost to time and affectionately remembered as it was colloquially called: Pisco John's. Duncan Nicol was John, and Pisco was his badge.

Was it just that the Pisco punch was so delicious, its ingredients a robust balance of liquids from three continents? Perhaps. But I venture it had as much to do with the Bank Exchange being heralded around the globe as one of the best rooms in which to raise a glass, to enjoy exquisite service, to see and be seen. In short, the Bank Exchange Saloon got it right: whatever happened within its walls was going to be talked about.

The Bank Exchange opened in 1853 and, according to Pauline Jacobson, a brilliant chronicler of the glamour and lore of early San Francisco, the saloon "always prepared punches with Pisco." Fast-forward forty years and a Scottish immigrant, a taciturn barber turned barman who had scraped together enough funds to buy the most desired saloon in the West, purchased the Bank Exchange from his boss and perfected its Pisco punch.

That Scotsman was Duncan Nicol, and Nicol made the punch famous. Resolute and terse, a man of impeccable taste, the fame of Pisco punch is attached to the command of this barman's persona.

Many have wondered if Nicol's creation was particularly potent. Most certainly it was.

In an era when cocktails were principally composed with fortified wines, aperitifs, and vermouths of every ilk, the Pisco punch was one of the first to turn this old formula upside down: the spirit became the principal ingredient. That was a novel idea then, and so the Pisco punch was extra, extra boozy. This potency prompted the resolute Scotsman of impeccable taste to institute a rule still found in some saloons today: only two drinks allowed per customer! (If you asked for a third, you were kindly told to exit, to walk around the Montgomery Block, and then to reapply for your position at the bar—should your condition be approved.) Nicol was also known to be rather protective of his intellectual property, his recipes; "Even Mr. Volstead himself could not pry the recipe from my lips," Nicol muttered in the midst of Prohibition.

As a fellow barman, I have long respected Nicol's wishes. But the catch is, Nicol bought the original recipe from the former owner, the Bank Exchange closed at the beginning of Prohibition, and Nicol passed away during those dark years. The City of San Francisco and bartenders across the globe have long yearned for the proper recipe to this notorious tipple. And so I along with others in San Francisco, in Peru, and around the globe took to researching this cocktail's origins and its final resting recipe.

For decades after Nicol's death, speculation on the contents of the fabled drink never ceased. Formulas were found scribbled on scraps of paper, quietly whispered in corner saloons, and printed in letters to local newspapers. Many thought that the magic ingredient in the punch was merely *gomme arabique*—"gum arabic"—the lovely ingredient employed to bind ingredients, thereby smoothing out any rough edges. Yes, gum arabic was used in the punch, as it was in many cocktails of that era. A great cocktail, like a great symphony, needs all of its instruments present and to play in balance.

* * *

My research into all of those instruments, er, ingredients, led me to one dramatic yet simple conclusion. I remembered the quote by Rudyard Kipling, who, after drinking a Pisco punch at the Bank Exchange, declared that the cocktail was "compounded of the shavings of cherub's wings, the glory of a tropical dawn, the red clouds of sunset and the fragments of lost epics by dead masters." In addition to Kipling's crimson description, there has long been a belief that the Pisco punch of ribald San Francisco had cocaine in it. (Horrors!) Of course, cocaine as we know it now didn't exist in 1893 during Nicol's tenure. So what could have made "a gnat fight an elephant," as Pauline Jacobson also quipped after drinking a Pisco punch? My conclusion is that it was the same thing that is enjoyed in cocktails and cuisine throughout Peru today: coca leaves.

I own the only unopened bottle of original Bank Exchange Pisco punch known to the world, which states on its front label, "According to the Original Formula of Duncan Nicol." The liquid contents inside this relic, though oxidized, have always been a reddish brown. This crimson color had previously perplexed me.

In 1893, the Bordeaux-produced Vin Mariani, a fortified, aromatized red wine infused with coca leaves, captivated the attention of the world. Developed in the 1860s by chemist and health expert Angelo Mariani, Vin Mariani harnessed the magic of the Incas—coca leaves—in his wildly popular aperitif. Soon, many more coca wines followed, being produced in Bordeaux and California alike. But just a decade after Mariani's colorful aperitif caught on, both the political climate for alcohol was souring and coca was being blamed for various undesirable behaviors. Soon, all coca wines were banned. Shortly before Prohibition, products containing actual coca could no longer be legally sold in the United States.

This would have been a strange, terrific blow to Nicol. To him, Vin Mariani was just a delicious red Bordeaux that added a nice lift, a beautiful color to his punch. He surely must have wondered why the authorities were up in arms. After all, both Thomas Edison and Pope Leo XIII had endorsed the healthful benefits of Angelo Mariani's creation.

In 1963, long after the Bank Exchange had been shuttered, with Nicol passed away and a whole generation of cocktailians not knowing what might have been in their Pisco punch before 1919, Lillet Rouge was introduced to the American market based on the prior success of fortified, aromatized wines from Bordeaux. Lillet, unable to use coca in its recipe, employs another botanical from Peru: cinchona bark, the progenitor of quinine. Lillet Rouge tastes as close to Vin Mariani as any aperitif of similar origin and production process ever could. Unfortunately, in 1963, Lillet Rouge did not launch its business in San Francisco by promoting its suitability for Pisco punch. That tradition had been forgotten, tucked away for this generation to discover.

Pisco, single distilled and bold, is rightly thought of as the white brown spirit. Add fresh-squeezed lime juice, an equal amount of a pineapple cordial with gum arabic in it, then the splash of Lillet Rouge and a nip of bitters, and this revived Pisco punch becomes a magical, deadly cocktail—just the kind you would like to order two, no three, rounds of, if the bartender is willing.

# PISCO, THE GRAND
# EAU-DE-VIE OF THE TROPICS

Pisco in San Francisco was a phenomenon, and it was this rich and unique history that led me down the rabbit hole into my two passions: to discover the untold stories of the cocktails of San Francisco and to produce Campo de Encanto Pisco in Peru.

For centuries before the Pisco punch became the signature cocktail of the Barbary Coast, the tropical eau-de-vie had been produced in the Viceroyalty of Peru, the sister territory to old California and the Viceroyalty of New Spain (Mexico). Francisco Pizarro's third effort to capture the gold of Peru began in 1530 in the port town of Sanlúcar de Barrameda, in the southwestern Spanish region of Jerez. After successfully entering the Andes and engaging in a few significant skirmishes, Pizarro began colonizing South America for the Spanish crown. The Jesuits and other colonists who accompanied him brought with them the strong, plentiful grape varieties of southern Spain and the Canary Islands.

For many centuries before the advent of electricity and climate-controlled wine cellars, the only way to preserve and protect wine from spoiling was to add a little aguardiente de vino, the distillate of young wine, blended back into the wine to fortify it for safekeeping. In 1575, the Spanish crown, frustrated by the success of wine production in the New World and its interference with the exportation of wine from Spain to the Americas, banned the production of wine in both Mexico and Peru. The plucky Peruvians, determined not to lose their vineyard assets, agreed to abide by the new rules, successfully inserting one single point in the negotiation: they would no longer produce wine, only aguardiente de vino. At the time, this exception was scoffed at, thought of as absurd. Peru immediately transitioned into a grape-distillate drinking culture.

The distilled spirit came to be called Pisco, as the best spirit of the Viceroyalty of Peru originated in the valley inland from that little port on Peru's Pacific coast. That it came north to San Francisco and became wildly popular is no accident. For centuries prior to the birth of San Francisco, Pisco was held aloft as the prized tipple of the New World, particularly along the Pacific. It was sought out by Sir Francis Drake as early as 1579, poured in the finest haciendas in Mexico City, and quaffed in Alta California long before the territory came into the United States.

In an old San Francisco directory of liquor dealers, bars, and wholesalers, I dug up a listing for a Pisco distillery in Napa, California, which seemed to have been in business as of 1850. I wondered, how would that have been possible? Gold had just been discovered, and California had but a few thousand people in the region. Perhaps the original Californians knew something that many have since forgotten: that the most commonly grown grape in Peru is known as Quebranta, which is identical to the Palomino Negro grape of Spain, and is the same vine as California's Mission grape, the first *Vitis vinifera* vine planted in the Americas. And did the Spanish of California simply adopt the word *Pisco* as the common, preferred term for aguardiente, or brandy, in the Pacific, which explains how their cousins farther south in Chile came to do so, as well? Whatever the truth may be, some fifty years later, Pisco boasted a long and storied history in California and the proprietor of the Bank Exchange Saloon was dubbed Pisco John. Nicol, like many great bartenders before and after him, stood on the shoulders of giants.

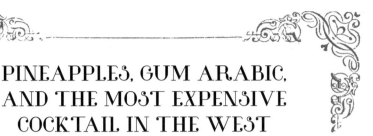

# PINEAPPLES, GUM ARABIC, AND THE MOST EXPENSIVE COCKTAIL IN THE WEST

There was a time before vast pineapple plantations made the fruit a commodity to be exported, when the tropical *ananá* was a rare and wonderful fruit whose image would become the international symbol of hospitality.

In the years immediately following the gold rush, San Francisco commanded all the pretty and delicious things the world had to offer. Ships stocked with Champagne from Le Havre, France, docked in the port, followed by vessels from Pisco, Peru, loaded with the indigenous fruits of South America that brought an even higher price than the coveted sparkling wine. The pineapple was regarded as a particularly bright and fragile delight, a treasure subject to bruising and full of sugar and tropical mystery.

Not surprisingly, Johnson, Boothby, and Nicol were seduced by the pineapple, making it an indispensible ingredient in the Pisco punch, the East India, and other drinks of local origin. It also contributed to the tab for Nicol's Pisco punch, which was four times the cost of any other cocktail.

Pineapple mixed with the principal spirits of the day—Pisco, rum, brandy, and whiskey—yielded drinks that were bright with foreign flavor. Having fresh pineapple syrup in your cocktail was an experience in decadence. It was frivolous, immortal fun, and the saloons that offered drinks with pineapple proudly displayed the mystery fruit in their front windows.

But pineapple wasn't the only thing that the savvy mixologists of the Barbary Coast regularly used to set their drinks apart. They also relied on gum arabic. What's that? you ask. Only a great secret about to be revealed! Gum arabic, or plain ol' gum, is made from the sap of certain species of acacia tree. It is most commonly processed into a powder, which, when mixed with water, becomes a thick, gelatinous, gummy solution. It is used in the food and drink industry, most commonly in candies, confections, and soft drinks, and is an old-time secret ingredient of the global wine business. Gum arabic acts as a stabilizer, a binding agent that not only causes tannins and proteins to unite but also smoothes out any rough edges in the process. A little gum goes a long way in a drink, creating a rich, smooth viscosity on the palate. The original cocktail slingers of the Barbary Coast knew that, so they all used it in their syrups, especially the most exotic and favored of the lot, pineapple.

## Homemade Pineapple Cordial

*By Scott Baird, courtesy of Trick Dog*

1 small ripe pineapple

2 cups/480 ml water

4 cups/800 g organic evaporated cane sugar

½ tsp salt

Peel and core the pineapple, then cut into half wheels 1 in/2.5 cm thick. Preheat a large nonstick frying pan over medium-high heat until hot but not smoking. Gently lay the pineapple half wheels in the hot pan and sear, turning once, until nicely browned on both sides, roughly 3 minutes on each side. Remove the pan from the heat and transfer the pineapple to a cutting board.

Return the pan to medium-high heat, add the water, and deglaze the pan, stirring gently to dislodge any browned solids on the pan bottom. Pour the contents of the frying pan into a saucepan, add the sugar and salt, place over high heat, and bring to a boil. While the mixture is heating, roughly chop the caramelized pineapple. Once the mixture is at a boil, turn the heat to low and skim off any foam from the surface. Carefully place the pineapple in the syrup and simmer gently for 10 minutes without stirring.

Remove from the heat and let cool completely, then strain through a chinois. Transfer to a tightly capped bottle or jar and store in a refrigerator for up to 4 weeks.

*Makes about 2 cups/480 ml*

*To Create a Gum Arabic Cordial: Only a little additional work is required to add gum arabic to your cordial. Add ½ cup/235 g powdered gum arabic just after you add the water. Once you turn the heat to low, stir the mixture thoroughly until the gum arabic is fully dissolved. Then skim off the foam and proceed as directed.*

## East India Cocktail
*By Harry Johnson*

1½ oz/45 ml Campo de Encanto
Grand & Noble Pisco

¾ oz/20 ml pineapple cordial,
homemade (see facing page) or
store-bought

½ oz/15 ml aged rum

½ oz/15 ml fresh lime juice

½ oz/15 ml fresh orange juice

2 dashes aromatic bitters, homemade
(see page 104) or store-bought

Expressed orange peel for garnish

Pour the liquid into a mixing glass, add
ice, shake, and strain into a chilled
cocktail glass. Garnish with the orange
peel.

## Single Village Fix
*By Thad Vogler, courtesy of Bar Agricole*

1½ oz/45 ml mezcal

¾ oz/20 ml fresh lime juice

¾ oz/20 ml pineapple cordial,
homemade (see facing page) or
store-bought

Pour the liquid into a mixing glass, add
ice, shake, and strain into a chilled
cocktail glass.

## The Misdemeanor
*By Duggan McDonnell*

2 to 3 serrano chile slices

2 oz/60 ml tequila blanco

1 oz/30 ml fresh lime juice

1 oz/30 ml pineapple cordial,
homemade (see facing page) or
store-bought

½ oz/15 ml green Chartreuse

Thin cucumber slice for garnish

Muddle the chile slices in a mixing glass,
add ice, then pour in the liquid and
shake vigorously. Strain into a highball
glass filled with ice and garnish with the
cucumber slice.

**NO. 4**

**THE HIGHBALL**

*Scotch + soda, vodka + soda, Campari + soda, and on and on*

## SCOTCH AND SODA

2 oz/60 ml blended Scotch,
such as Great King Street or Sheep Dip

2 oz/60 ml seltzer

Pour the liquid into a highball glass. Add ice, swirl, and smile.

The Scotch and soda, the most venerable of highballs, is still served at plenty of watering holes throughout the City. It is a gentleman's aperitif—an aperitif in the nonprescriptive way, the way a great, simple drink can make you feel better about your life. It's never fussy, always delivers. That's the genius of the highball.

These days, the highball has become a thrown-around, cheapened catchall term for a drink in a tall glass. It isn't, however. A highball is a specific, nongeneric beverage of equal parts distilled greatness and effervescence, and if you're drinking one in the Big 4 Restaurant atop Nob Hill as I do from time to time, that means Scotch and soda.

Across the land, the highball has been largely replaced by the ubiquitous vodka served with soda. To a mixologist, that's an abhorrent call. The only equivalent I can think of for a chef would be if a diner ordered pasta plus rice, hold the sauce. No disrespect to vodka or to pasta; both have their place.

You can change the principal spirit to Campari, tequila, or gin, but if you add a freshly squeezed lime, the drink becomes a rickey.

Here in the Big 4, a Scotch and soda at the bantam-size bar is the perfect highball, made perfectly. The Big 4 is on the bottom floor of the famed Huntington Hotel, so named for the four enterprising fellows who changed the economic and popular course of American history by creating the first transcontinental railroad. Charles Crocker, Mark Hopkins, Collis Huntington, and Leland Stanford financed the Central Pacific Railroad that bridged connecting railways from the West across the country, allowing travelers to leave Grand Central Terminal and arrive at the San Francisco Bay just eight days later. Then, as now, whiskey holds a place in American drinking, and Scotch, being so venerated, imported, is the perfect tipple to enjoy in the Big 4.

These days, with a whiskey boom in full swing, many delightful and ingenious blends of Scotch are available. This is the quintessential way to drink Scotch, a profound and whimsical liquid blended by a master, lightly opened with an equal amount of seltzer, and served over a single stone of ice.

Still seated at that little bar, I slowly sip my perfect Scotch and soda and watch as a man in a well-worn tuxedo approaches the piano in the corner. He sits down cautiously yet comfortably, as if he's in his living room, and then begins to play "Yesterdays," just as Artie Shaw once did. Distilled greatness has never tasted so effervescent.

# ON EFFERVESCENCE

The majority of spirits in the United States are consumed in cocktails, that is, in some form of mixed drink, and the simplest form of the mixed drink is some type of spirit and water. Adding sparkling water—seltzer, soda water, or mineral water—to a spirit is my preferred method of enjoying a lighter drinking experience. Beyond the simple dilution that such an addition brings to the glass, sparkling water—if it is from a mineral spring—naturally has both a high mineral content and tiny bubbles. Both of these aspects can often make a distilled spirit taste lighter, if not better.

In the case of Scotch, which can taste of salinity, or just a little bit of salt, the minerality in the water adds a pleasant structure to the beverage, while the bubbles open and lift the flavor molecules to the top of the drink.

# THE NEGRONI
## NO. 5

*Inspired by Count Camillo Negroni, created by Fosco Scarselli, and very dear to San Francisco's heart*

## NEGRONI

1 oz/30 ml No. 209 gin

1 oz/30 ml Italian vermouth

1 oz/30 ml Campari

Expressed orange peel for garnish

Pour the liquid into a mixing glass, add ice, stir forty times, then strain into a highball glass filled with ice cubes. Garnish with the orange peel and sip and sigh.

The Negroni is San Francisco's most-beloved cocktail import. In this case, the City, which usually plays the role of vanguardist, had the good sense to embrace something so wonderful and seemingly so very foreign. The ultimate San Francentric cocktail, the bright, bitter, and boozy Negroni was created in the land of Da Vinci.

I have known native San Franciscans who have spent their lives, far into their winter years, always drinking Negronis, such is the love for and dedication to the drink. In April 2013, I was quoted in the *New York Times* as saying, "This town loves its Negronis!" Throughout the region, from the coast of Mendocino down to the bay of Monterey, the Negroni is the most ubiquitous cocktail of historic origin. And it's tough going to get a bad one.

Part of its success is due to the simplicity of the recipe: equal parts gin, sweet vermouth, and the historic amaro of Milan, Campari. These days, most bar folks pour a shot and a half each from their three selected bottles into a mixing glass, stir, strain into a chilled coupe, and then finish with a freshly expressed orange peel. A few know to pour the drink into a tall glass over ice, as they do in Milan, to preserve the bold aperitif just a little bit longer.

In Gaz Regan's book *The Negroni*, Robert Simonson writes, "Within that three-decker arrangement, the Negroni manages to bring every taste bud into play. The gin provides its varied botanical bite. The Vermouth lends a bit of sweet, a bit of spicy. Most critically, Campari brings on the bitter so beloved by a barkeep's sophisticated palate. Whatever sensation you're looking for in your cocktail, it's in there. It is that dichotomy of variety within purity that bewitches so many. Moreover, the Negroni gives each of these challenging ingredients its chance to shine. No member of the trio dominates. All have their say. The Negroni is a democracy."

I wrote that the Negroni is an imported notion, a foreigner in San Francisco, and that its bright, bitter booziness became a ubiquitous delight. But that reality in no way diminishes its small, authentic origin in the City. Campari, in fact, gained a foothold here before its preeminent cocktail did. A Campari with soda, the first local riff on the highball, was the drink of choice of my wife's grandmother, Frances Lent, and her gaggle of girlfriends in the 1940s. At the time, Frances, a good-looking gal with a great set of pipes, sang at Shanghai Lil on Kearny Street, where she entertained soldiers home from the war. Before the music started, Frances and her friends would gather and each would sip a Campari with soda. Then, with the room flush with soldiers and the piano player at his keyboard, Frances would sit atop the grand piano and sing to the crowd. One night, a young Michael Sanchez, still wearing his naval uniform—because it was the nicest thing he owned—listened in awe as Frances sang. For Michael, it was love at first sight, and so exhibiting the pluck that came to define his persona, he said aloud "I'm gonna marry that gal!"

Between sets, and before she could rejoin her girlfriends, Frances was approached by the young navy man, who offered to buy her and her friends a round of those tall, crimson delights. The bottle of Campari was emptied, and so began my wife's grandparents' first date.

The Negroni is a much more serious alcoholic concoction than Frances's glowing, slightly bitter highball. But it was not until the next decade that San Franciscans—mostly men, you see, who were the type to order a Manhattan—began barking for the boozy Negroni. The tradition started in the Italian restaurants of North Beach, and within a few decades, the Negroni became the house drink at Alfred's Steakhouse. Art Petri bought the joint in 1973, and when Alfred's longtime customers saw Art and his son Al drinking tall Negronis as if they were glasses of water fresh from the Hetch Hetchy Reservoir, those Manhattan drinkers traded in their bourbon. The most popular happy hour in town became packed with three-piece suits doing deals over round after round of Negronis.

In the twenty-first century, a fitting place as any to enjoy a Negroni is in the renovated Tosca Café on Columbus Avenue, not far from Montgomery Street—smack in the middle of the Devil's Acre. Jeannette Etheredge, the grand dame of San Francisco's bar scene for decades, sold Tosca to superchef April Bloomfield, a grand dame herself, in 2013. The transition has been a smooth one: when you step through the front door, the romance of Tosca has been perfectly preserved. Sitting along its winding, oval bar, the sense of history is palpable. The barmen dressed in white coats are not an example of shtick; no, that's heritage, and as they move busily behind the wood, one understands right away the reverence for good drink.

"Negroni. 209 gin. Tall, please," I bark above the din. "San Francisco style." The City's smartest and finest have long gathered here, and thanks to the recent Bloomfield push, even more so. The barman making my Negroni tells me he's new in town, just in from New Orleans. For a split second, this bit of conversation has me nervous. But he's a splendid talent, regaling me as he pours. Just as I requested, a bit of salt falls from his fingertips, then he stirs, strains, and delivers the delight to me.

I sip. This Negroni is light, bitter, softly savory, and highly aromatic. Perfectly chilled, it also boasts a refreshing quality that few all-booze tipples can match. The sweet vermouth delivers a lovely viscosity that transcends any offense encountered from the attack of the alcohol. And the salt? That just makes everything more interesting. Within this conundrum, how can a San Franciscan, or any sophisticated cocktail drinker, balk at this delight? The Negroni had San Francisco in its grasp long before it arrived.

The night is coming on, as more and more headlights flick and then rush past the window shutters facing Columbus Avenue. My glass is empty, only ice remains. "Hey, barkeep!" I holler in jest. "If you're able to repeat your success, I'd be most appreciative."

# OUR BITTERSWEET AFFAIR

In cities with a robust culinary culture, a vibrant exchange of ingredients and ideas, a digestif is often taken after a meal: A nip of raki in Istanbul, Armagnac in Paris, Fernet-Branca in San Francisco. This tradition of enjoying a distilled spirit upon finishing the eating portion of the meal is designed to soften the palate, to temper the weight of the food in the stomach by cutting through fat and protein, and to aid digestion. The best digestifs—those specifically designed to the task—are typically herb-and-spice-heavy infusions and quite bitter on the palate. These tonic liquors are also primarily of Italian origin, so they are generally referred to by their Italian term, amaro and amari, singular and plural respectively. (The word *amaro* translates to "bitter" in Italian.) San Francisco is a city of gourmands, trenchermen, and scofflaws; with so much eating and drinking going on, a prescriptive amaro is often in order.

The typical amaro is boldly flavored and fantastically bitter, with flavors of cardamom, mint, saffron, quassia bark, and rhubarb. Often times, caramel is added to the final blend before bottling to ease the burden of the medicine on the palate.

Two brands of amari are embraced in the City above all others, and both are from Milan: Fernet-Branca and Campari. San Francisco received a large number of immigrants from northern Italy in the first half of the twentieth century. They brought with them their recipes for Tuscan dishes, their wines from Umbria, their love of chocolate. And with such a rich diet, they also enjoyed their daily ration of their preferred amaro. Campari was often consumed during the day, mixed with soda as an aperitif, and the very bold Fernet-Branca was taken after a hearty meal in the evening. I'm told that these bottles lived on kitchen tables and in the cafés of North Beach, from which they migrated over

Russian Hill into Cow Hollow and the Marina, where they were soon found on back bars. By World War II, these brands were typical staples of every good saloon in San Francisco. Just as Italian food and wine became ubiquitous throughout San Francisco, so too did these amari.

These days, it's chic to slug back shots of Fernet-Branca or to arrive to a party with a bottle of Campari tucked beneath your arm. But before this current trend, drinking an amaro was a simple and sophisticated thing to do.

As I've noted, a port city receives foods and flavors before its neighboring terrains, so it is often the first to develop a more international palate. My research led me to a particular conclusion: San Francisco's passion for amari is to be traced not just to the arrival of Italian immigrants and to a palate formed by the intersection of bold, spiced cuisines from Asia and Latin America but also to its countless cafés and tea shops. For more than 150 years, many different tannic brews have been consumed daily in San Francisco. In other words, this is a city of passionate tea and coffee drinkers, and that culture has in turn produced many local tea and coffee companies that are now known throughout the country. Today, the Port of Oakland receives more imported coffee beans and bulk tea than any other port in the world.

Decades ago, if you were to walk along the Embarcadero, the bold aroma of the Hill Bros. factory roasting its coffee beans would accompany your stroll. The scent of salt from the sea, roasting beans, and dishes from many lands has permeated San Francisco since its earliest day. Those aromas primed the palate of the average San Franciscan for amaro consumption. To some people, an amaro may be too bitter, too astringent, too medicinal. But if you begin your day with an espresso and a breakfast of huevos rancheros, then stop for a Hong Kong–style clay pot and some black tea for lunch, sip a cocktail in the late afternoon, and enjoy pasta with Dungeness crab for dinner, capping the day with an amaro is a natural progression. And in San Francisco, you can easily do all of that in one day—on a single block!

*Fireside Lounge on Nob Hill, March 10, 1943*

## 1794

*By Dominic Venegas, courtesy of NoMad, New York City*

2 oz/60 ml rye whiskey

1 oz/30 ml Italian vermouth

1 oz/30 ml Campari

Expressed orange peel for garnish

Pour the liquid into a mixing glass, add ice, stir forty times, then strain into a cocktail glass and garnish with the orange peel.

## Intercontinental

*By Duggan McDonnell*

1½ oz/45 ml Cognac

1 oz/30 ml Averna

¼ oz/10 ml maraschino liqueur

Expressed orange peel for garnish

Pour the liquid into a mixing glass, add ice, stir forty times, then strain into a cocktail glass and garnish with the orange peel.

## Jasmine

*By Paul Harrington, courtesy of Enrico's Sidewalk Café*

1½ oz/45 ml gin

1 oz/30 ml Cointreau or other orange curaçao

¾ oz/20 ml Campari

½ oz/15 ml fresh lemon juice

Expressed orange peel for garnish

Pour the liquid into a mixing glass, add ice, shake, then fine-strain into a cocktail glass and garnish with the orange peel.

# NO. 6

## THE IRISH COFFEE

*Plucked from Ireland by Jack Koeppler and Stan Delaplane and made perfect on the shore of the San Francisco Bay*

## IRISH COFFEE

1½ oz/45 ml Tullamore D.E.W. Irish whiskey

1 Tbsp superfine sugar

3 oz/90 ml hot brewed coffee

1 oz/30 ml heavy whipping cream

Pour the whiskey into an Irish coffee glass, add the sugar, and pour in the coffee. Stir quickly, float a "collar" of cream on the surface by layering it over the back of a spoon atop the coffee, and then savor the warmth.

It is a cold and drizzly day on the north end of San Francisco. We are in the first week of March and the February rains are still with us. The atmosphere is thick, wet, and gray; a foghorn sounds, warning the incoming tankers that the old prison Alcatraz lies in their way. Sheltered from the damp is everyone inside the Buena Vista, which stands where Hyde Street ends at Beach, where the cable car finds the sea after conquering several hills, its route ending just a few steps from the doors of the café.

More than fifty of us are sitting on bar stools and at tables, yet the mood is subdued. "It's quiet today," chimes in Nicholas from behind the wood. I have to agree with Nick, my last visit to the Buena Vista was on Black Friday, and I was playing host-cum-tour guide to visiting relatives. They had told me that a visit to Fog City wouldn't be complete without drinking an Irish coffee, and so we headed to the famed café. It was jammed to the gills, with steam on all of the windows obscuring the view of the Golden Gate. It seemed as if at least two hundred people were there that day, with so much laughter that you couldn't hear yourself or anyone else speak. And everyone seemed to be holding the same thing: the footed tulip, three-quarters dark with a collar of cream about its top.

I am sitting with Jane Maher, an Irish lass from County Kilkenny by way of Trinity College. Jane is the ambassador for Tullamore D.E.W. Irish whiskey, and she has spent quite a few afternoons here on Hyde Street.

"I spent twelve hours here one Saturday," Jane says to me. "Irish Coffee Day, it was. And it was one of the best days of my life."

I admit to Jane that I didn't realize that the Irish coffee had its own day of celebration (it's in July), and I'm surprised to learn that it wasn't conceived by the owners of the Buena Vista. But Jane isn't taken in by my bait. "It's the people who come in here," she continues, "the most interesting people."

Admittedly, Jane is obligated to spend a lot of time here in the Buena Vista, the home of the Irish coffee and the largest purchaser of Tullamore D.E.W. whiskey in the world. We sip our Irish coffees slowly and continue to chat. The drink, it seems, is a perfect fit to the weather outside and to whatever mood is brewing inside. It is certainly a cocktail—if it can be called such—that demands the occasion of conversation. Served piping hot, it cannot be slammed down one's gullet. Nor is it served tall with a straw to allow quick sipping. No, the Irish coffee demands that the drinker take his or her time, and so the occasion of conversation presents itself.

This same experience has been happening here on the north—the grayest—side of the City for over sixty years, since Jack Koeppler and Stan Delaplane, proprietor and journalist, respectively, set out to create a drink that was much more than whiskey and coffee. And they succeeded. Jane orders a second Irish coffee for me, and I watch as Saint Nick, who has been behind-the-stick at the Buena Vista for four years now, lines up the tulip glasses and begins to pour. His white barman's jacket holds a curious sludge of stain on the right forearm, born from the pouring of tens of thousands of Irish coffees. The same is true of his left hand, all of his fingertips are dark from holding glass after glass as he pours the coffee and thousands of little splashes make their way beneath his fingernails. A true craftsman, Nick makes every Irish coffee perfectly, the same singular drink.

I bring mine to my lips; sweet cream it is, and beneath it comes a hot, slightly boozy, somewhat sweet coffee. The ingredients are perfectly integrated, balanced. You might not realize that a few fingers of whiskey are in every glass. I suddenly notice that Jane doesn't have a drink in front of her. How rude of me, I think to myself.

"Are you not having another drink?" I ask.

"I am not having another drink," she responds, with a twinkle in her eye. "But I will have another Irish coffee. Nick?"

*Bartenders making Irish coffees at the Buena Vista Cafe, 1973*

# ON COFFEE & COCKTAILS

To call a drink composed of alcohol, sugar, cream, and coffee a cocktail is a stretch. It could be called a tipple, a shim, or just dessert. Unlike the Irish coffee, such concoctions are typically too sweet, too fatty, too gas inducing. Most discriminating drinkers will turn up their nose at boozy beverages made with coffee, and for good reason.

But like the Irish coffee, there are also a few good ones. Perhaps you've heard of, or even tried, a Spanish coffee? I certainly have. I've poured at least a few hundred in my day, too. The Spanish coffee is a delicious treat, certainly decadent, and something to enjoy when you want to splurge, you're not taking yourself too seriously, and all the cameras have been put away. You see, the Spanish coffee involves fire—real fire. And that single fact accounts for most of the Spanish coffees ordered these days: people always like a good show.

For quite a while, I tried to find the answer as to when coffee and booze were first put together in such a combustible fashion, but I was unsuccessful. And then, after one particular shift at Absinthe Brasserie &

Bar, I ceased trying. It was a Saturday night, the opera crowd had just arrived after the performance, and the place was packed. The bar was crowded with groups ordering Sazeracs, and the dining room was equally busy with tables requesting Spanish coffees for dessert. Now, these two drinks share a similar technique: glasses are swirled in each hand to coat their interiors with respective alcohols. The Sazerac calls for swirling absinthe in the glass and then flipping it aside. The Spanish coffee demands a careful spinning of the glass as the overproof rum, all afire, burns on its inside, crystallizing the sugar about its rim.

Well, on this very busy Saturday night, I was working as fast as I could and muscle memory failed me: rather than tossing out the few drops of absinthe from the Sazerac glass in my right hand, I was, in fact, making a Spanish coffee and flung a couple of shots of blazing 151 rum onto the floor and up the back bar. A long streak of extremely hot and still-burning rum clung to the wood, so I threw body over flame to squelch it, just before the crowd started to stare and the whole place burned down. I haven't made a Spanish coffee since.

Of course, I've enjoyed alcoholic drinks with coffee, usually an espresso with a nip of Pisco or something equally simple. But in times past, I have enjoyed the counterpart to the very famous house cappuccino at Tosca, the white nun. The drink, which was a clever pun on the darker coffee cocktail and its namesake, the Capuchin fathers, was always popular with the ladies who worked beneath the neon and in the dark corners of the Devil's Acre, who appreciated the irony when enjoying the tipple. The white nun, like the house cappuccino, has a bit of chocolate in it, inspired by the northern Italians who once populated the neighborhood.

Whichever version of coffee spiked with booze and sweetened you like, the weather in San Francisco is perfect for such concoctions. You'll appreciate its rousing warmth hitting your chest and its caffeine perking you up just a bit before stepping back out into the wind and fog.

## Spanish Coffee

*Courtesy of Absinthe Brasserie & Bar*

Superfine sugar

1 oz/30 ml overproof rum

Pinch of ground cinnamon

4 oz/120 ml hot brewed coffee

½ oz/15 ml coffee liqueur

½ oz/15 ml California brandy

Dollop of whipped cream for garnish

Coat the rim of a heat-resistant glass by wetting the glass and then dipping it into a plate of superfine sugar. Pour the overproof rum into the glass and ignite the rum. As the alcohol burns, slowly twist the glass, lowering and raising the liquid in it. As you turn the glass, sprinkle in the cinnamon. As the flame burns itself out, pour in the coffee, liqueur, and brandy. Top with the cream.

## The White Nun

*By Isaac Shumway, Courtesy of Tosca Café*

¾ oz/20 ml Straus Family Creamery whipping cream, plus more cream for topping the drink

¾ oz/20 ml Straus Family Creamery whole milk

1 bar spoon (⅛ oz/5 ml) Cold Brew Coffee Syrup (facing page)

1 oz/30 ml St. George Nola coffee liqueur

½ oz/15 ml Marie Duffau Napoléon Bas Armagnac

Pour the cream, milk, and coffee syrup into an Irish coffee glass. Steam with a steam wand until hot. Froth some additional cream with the steam wand and let rest while you finish the drink. Add the liqueur and Armagnac to the hot milk mixture and stir briefly. Top with the foamed cream to taste.

# Cold Brew Coffee Syrup

2 vanilla beans

3 cups/600 g sugar

1 cup/240 ml hot water

12 oz/340 g coarsely ground coffee
(ground for French press)

Halve each vanilla bean lengthwise, then,
using the tip of a knife, scrape the seeds
from the beans into a container large
enough to hold all of the ingredients. Add
the sugar, pour in the water, and stir to
dissolve the sugar. Let cool completely,
add the coffee, and stir to mix well. Cover
and let stand at room temperature for
24 hours.

Strain the mixture through a fine-mesh
sieve, pressing against the coffee grounds
to extract as much syrup as possible.
Transfer to an airtight container and
refrigerate. The syrup will keep for up
to 4 weeks.

*Makes about 4 cups/1 L*

# THE
# SCORPION BOWL

*Created by Trader Vic Bergeron*
*for willing fools everywhere*

## SCORPION BOWL

6 oz/180 ml white rum

6 oz/180 ml fresh orange juice

4 oz/120 ml fresh lemon juice

1½ oz/45 ml orgeat syrup, homemade (see page 55) or store-bought

1 oz/30 ml brandy

Mint sprig and orange, lemon, and lime wheels for garnish

Have ready two pitchers. Pour all the liquid into one pitcher, add crushed ice, and then roll the contents between the two pitchers four times. Pour the contents into a large ceramic scorpion bowl, top with additional fresh ice, garnish with the mint and citrus wheels, and steady yourself.

The scorpion may be the most aptly named cocktail in a book titled *Drinking the Devil's Acre*. With a recipe that calls for serving up the ruination—7 ounces/210 millilitres of distilled spirit—in a "bowl," without the aid of friends, a scorpion bowl will, in fact, ruin the drinker.

When one meanders through the historic Fairmont Hotel, which sits majestically atop Nob Hill, what comes to mind is not how one will soon be ruined by drink. Yet the Fairmont is not only an elegant hospice in the City but also the place to get lost in a scorpion bowl. To find one, I ride the escalator down from the lobby to where the coral-colored halls end at the Tonga Room. As I enter, the quality of light shifts from bright and warm to dark and strange, and then turning and turning again, I find my way into the wonderfully weird nightclub dressed in Polynesian kitsch. The atmosphere is due to two deceased Californian restaurateurs' imaginations of what Pacific island culture never was: Trader Vic and Donn Beach created this aesthetic shortly after the demise of Prohibition, making it famous in Los Angeles, San Francisco, and beyond.

I take a seat at a low rattan table and order the specialty, the scorpion bowl. I do so because, well, I must. Am I a glutton for punishment? Am I planning to take the next two days off? Usually not, and certainly no. I must, in fact, be a functioning adult tomorrow.

Suddenly, there is an auditory boom, a thunderous clap, and then a flash of light. Again it comes, the cycle repeats. I look around inside the faux Polynesian island nightclub, and as my vision adjusts to the darkness, I begin to hear, then see rainfall. As I spy into the darkness, I recognize a giant moat just beyond my perch. The downpour continues—a perfect tropical storm from the darkened sky of the Tonga Room.

My scorpion bowl arrives and I nod in appreciation, or is it apprehension? The ceramic bowl chock-full of who knows what is punctuated with two giant straws beckoning my participation. I steady my nerves and mutter, "There's no way, no goddamn way I'm finishing this drink." I look around to see if anyone is watching the single guy, alone, in the dark room during a thunderstorm about to slurp a scorpion bowl. No one is looking my way except for the bartender, an older Filipino fellow in a bright blue Polynesian shirt who is also surveying the room. His gaze locks on me, the lone man with the biggest drink, the most potent punch in the room. The expression on his face is sublime, all knowing. He's seen this scenario before, and he knows what's going to happen next.

Indignant and determined, I bite at the end of a straw, and after a quick sucking, several swallows flow down my gullet. I look back toward the bartender, but he's gone.

\*\*\*

Cocktail lore has it that the scorpion was likely first invented in a Honolulu bar called the Hut. Trader Vic got a consulting gig that took him to Hawaii, and while he was there, he did a little barhopping that included a stop at the Hut, where he encountered the first iteration of the scorpion. How he took the name and/or the recipe and made it his own is not known. Soon enough, however, the scorpion bowl had fully entered Trader Vic's drink list. What was the ingredient that made the scorpion a staple of the Trader's repertoire? Orgeat syrup.

A well-made scorpion bowl boasts the same delightful balance as three other drinks of local origin: the mai tai (page 53), the East India Cocktail (page 71), and the fogcutter (page 56). That's because each includes freshly squeezed citrus and either the combination of cane- and grape-based distillates or the use of orgeat syrup—ingredients that Vic regularly employed.

***

Sitting in the Tonga Room, I wish I could fully appreciate the mixological delight in front of me as exactly that. But my tongue has gone numb, as have my limbs. Is that why these two long straws are a feature of the scorpion bowl? So that the drinker can lean his weight forward and bob his mouth at the straws in order to keep sucking?

I look over at my bartender friend, but now there are two of him. His twin must have just arrived on shift. I mumble something to the waiter, the check arrives, and somehow I manage to pay my tab.

The beauty of leaving the Tonga Room is that when you exit the Fairmont on California Street, you are within stumbling distance of many of San Francisco's finest hotels. Heading down Nob Hill, gravity works in the drinker's favor.

Am I suggesting that after drinking a scorpion bowl that your night may be over? I most certainly am.

*The Ladies, Barbary Coast, 1890*

# ON SHARING DRINKS
# OR HOW TO USE A LONG STRAW

The scorpion bowl is clearly a cocktail designed to be shared. Sitting alone in the dark of the Tonga Room, slurping back plenty of alcohol from an oversize bowl, had me feeling more than just a little buzzed. Sad, lonely, weirdo—these are the descriptors that come to mind when I reflect on such an experience.

Punch bowls and cocktail pitchers are meant to be shared, offering a great way to both build community and have a little fun. That same philosophy marks the success of the tiki craze: beyond its silliness, frivolity, and kitsch, tiki promotes a culture of participation, of sharing. To sit at a little table together, to lean in and suck back so much sweet fun is an indispensible part of the tiki tradition. Without that aspect of sharing, tiki culture would be all style and no substance.

California, because of its long connection with Latin America, has always enjoyed shared punches. The ritual of punch in Latin America and in the Barbary Coast is decidedly different from, say, that of Great Britain and its colonies. Punch in the tropics never meant exactly five ingredients. In centuries past, at bullfights and in the theaters and taverns of Lima or Mexico City, citrus and other local fruits came together with spirit and wine in heady concoctions that overflowed big ceramic bowls. This tradition came to Alta California, to San Francisco. It wasn't just the Bank Exchange Saloon that featured punch on the Barbary Coast. Every bar along the Cocktail Route proudly poured from the house bowl.

In the years immediately following World War II, the tiki craze blossomed in the West and thrived for decades. Then, in the 1980s, sharing pitchers of sangria and margaritas took center stage in group drinking. The growth in immigrants from Latin America saw the opening of many new restaurants spread its culture. Everyone was happy to sit around a big table covered with platters of Latin food and pitchers of margaritas, all for sharing.

Although the wild punches of the Barbary Coast, this tiki-inspired scorpion bowl, and outsize margarita pitchers may no longer be as popular as they once were, the culture of sharing a drink in San Francisco has never gone out of style.

The Manhattan

No. 8

*Created by Dr. Ian Marshall,
New York City, and beloved by Fog City*

# MANHATTAN

1½ oz/45 ml Old Potrero rye whiskey

¾ oz/20 ml Italian vermouth

3 dashes aromatic bitters, homemade (see page 104)
or store-bought

Brandied cherry or expressed orange peel for garnish

Pour the liquid into a mixing glass, add ice, stir forty times,
then strain into a cocktail coupe and garnish with
either the cherry or the orange peel.

The Pied Piper bar in the Palace Hotel is the spiritual home of the Manhattan here on the Left Coast. The Manhattan was the signature cocktail bespoke by the master "Cocktail Bill" Boothby when he held forth within this glorious room after its reopening (following the earthquake and fire) in 1907. Boothby so loved his Manhattans that he couldn't help tinkering with the boozy delight. His evolution of this fabled cocktail inside the Palace drew the crème of San Francisco to New Montgomery Street, seven blocks south of the Bank Exchange Saloon, to sip what became known as the Boothby cocktail. What did Boothby do to his Manhattan? He finessed a smart play on the proportions and added a splash of the finest Champagne.

The best hour to climb atop a stool in the Pied Piper, your elbows comfortable on the old wooden bar top as you stare up at the original Maxfield Parrish painting above it, is precisely when the bar opens: 11:30 A.M. You'll order a Manhattan, or if you're one of the folks in the know, you'll ask for a Boothby cocktail. As the barkeep stirs your drink, take the time to reminisce on how one of history's great barmen stirred this same drink in this same room beneath the same Parrish painting. By 11:37, you've had several perfect sips of your Boothby and your day is already seeming a lot brighter.

\* \* \*

In February 1998, I was living in Seattle, where I spent one spontaneous night meeting and then traversing the downtown with three women from New York City. We dropped into a little *bohème* joint called the Pink Door. There was a stage, though no one sang. There were mismatched sofas of Victorian origin, marble-topped tables, and chandeliers, and the waitresses bore artisanal tattoos on their arms. The three ladies, Rosalie, Paige, and Justine, and I sat down on one of those Victorian couches and each of them chimed up, one after the other: "Maker's Mark Manhattan, please." My order was less alliterative: "The same."

I was twenty-three years old at the time and didn't know what a Maker's Mark Manhattan was. Was it similar to a Harvey Wallbanger or a Long Island iced tea? I wondered. Then again, in 1998, I didn't know what those cocktails were either.

The thoroughly tattooed waitress arrived with a tray of four large, brown yet bracingly clear cocktail glasses and set them on the table before us. Then together, we raised those Manhattans to our mouths. I endeavored to do so in such a way so as to appear experienced, though I very much felt a virgin. The ladies each took a demure sip, then set their respective cocktails down and picked up the conversation where it had left off. But, I . . . I did not. My Manhattan remained gripped in my hand, held aloft, floating just below my chin as the sweet and chilled burn coated my tongue and then ran down through my chest and tickled my toes. Oh, the Manhattan! I remained that way, a bit wide-eyed, I imagine, and altogether enlightened. I dared not have another sip, fearing the magic that lay inside the glass. But then, sensing that Rosalie, Paige, and Justine wouldn't notice, I nearly bit at the side of the glass, opened my mouth wide, and poured back the delight, gulping down the whiskey, vermouth, and bitters.

Until that moment inside the Pink Door, I had understood a cocktail to be something of juice, both tall and cloying, and never something bracing, never boozy yet altogether balanced, never enlightening and delicious. In that moment, I sensed, and then understood, that a change had taken place and that I was no longer the same man. I ordered another Manhattan, then a third. I picked up the tab and later exited the Pink Door taller than when I had arrived. In that unforeseen sip, I had learned to drink; something was given to me and something else was taken away. I laughed to myself, thinking, sensing that I was just a bit older, more experienced. I went to bed that night wondering what great moments lay ahead, still tasting that perfect cocktail, that Manhattan.

\* \* \*

Inside the Palace, the Pied Piper leads the way. You've had several Boothbys during the early lunch hour and each has gone to your head. The Champagne lifts the whiskey to the very tippy top of your brain and then sticks around to dance a bit more. Cocktail lore says that the Boothby was created right here at the height of the woman's suffrage movement, just before Prohibition. The Palace always hosted the most famous in the land—politicians of every sort, renowned actors and wealthy railroad barons, men and women alike. The Boothby cocktail suited its environs. It was a gorgeous sight to behold, and, most important, a drink that all could agree on, sip after decadent sip.

## Boothby Cocktail
*By "Cocktail Bill" Boothby*

1 oz/30 ml American whiskey

1 oz/30 ml Italian vermouth

Dash orange bitters

Dash aromatic bitters, homemade (see page 104) or store-bought

1½ oz/45 ml sparkling wine

Expressed orange peel for garnish

Pour the whiskey, vermouth, and both bitters into a mixing glass, add ice, stir forty times, then strain into a cocktail coupe. Top with the sparkling wine, stir lightly again, and delicately garnish the masterpiece with the orange peel.

## Prize Filly
*By Duggan McDonnell*

1½ oz/45 ml rye whiskey

½ oz/15 ml Punt e Mes vermouth

½ oz/15 ml maraschino liqueur

3 dashes orange bitters

3 dashes aromatic bitters, homemade (see page 104) or store-bought

Expressed orange peel for garnish

Pour the liquid into a mixing glass, add ice, stir forty times, then strain into a cocktail coupe and garnish with the orange peel.

## Revolver
*By Jon Santer, courtesy of Prizefighter*

2 oz/60 ml bourbon

½ oz/15 ml coffee liqueur

2 dashes orange bitters

Expressed orange peel for garnish

Pour the liquid into a mixing glass, add ice, stir forty times, then strain into a cocktail coupe and garnish with the orange peel.

# AROMATIC BITTERS:

## JUST A DASH FOR HEALTH AND FOR TASTE

In the early days of San Francisco, the local bars and restaurants were lousy with bitters. Everywhere you looked, handbills advertised commercial bitters that promised to cure your ills and delight you at the same time. Not surprisingly, the fast-growing city at the edge of the Pacific attracted some of the brightest apothecary minds in the world, along with a few charlatans. Salutaris Bitters, Cholera Antidote Bitters, African Stomach Bitters, Cassin's Grape Brandy Bitters, Old Dr. Rosenbaum's Bitters, McManman's Celebrated Stomach Bitters, Hostetter's Bitters, Lacour's Sarsaparaphere Bitters, Alex von Humboldt's Celebrated Stomach Bitters, Dr. Boerhaave's Celebrated Stomach Bitters, and Calisaya Bitters—all were among the commercially successful bitters of the day, all of them produced in San Francisco.

Bitters are essentially concoctions come together by the maceration of herbs, roots, and spices in alcohol to extract their virtues; it's then easier for the imbiber to receive any medicinal benefit from the various herbs after a slug or three of the bitters. They can be extraordinarily bitter on the palate, or they can be sweetened and taste rather like a spiced liqueur. In this case, the word *bitters* refers to the ingredients rather the final product.

Young San Francisco was a boomtown whose denizens held much disposable income and in which drinking what you liked was a way of life—a privilege that was enjoyed from early morning until night. However, disease was rampant, and the water not yet pure. Long before Mary Poppins sang that a spoonful of sugar helps a bit of medicine go down the gullet, the residents and mixologists of San Francisco understood that the pharmacy and the saloon were connected. On the Barbary Coast, men took their medicine like a man does and should, in a glass full of something delicious and intoxicating. The lively mix of so many cultures and customs and the offloading of the many flavors of the world onto the docks meant that drinking delicious bitters for health (and fun) began almost immediately in San Francisco, and it has not slowed since. Indeed, the early popularity of locally bottled bitters undoubtedly lead to the City's later love affair with amari (see page 80).

Barkeeps these days curate a lovely selection of bitters made around the world and also feature their own concoctions made in-house. But the foundation of bitters, we should all remember, is not only how they taste; it is also how they improve and revitalize the drinker's day. Nick Kosevich, cofounder of the Bittercube line of cocktail bitters and bar savant for San Mateo's Mortar & Pestle, shared with me the following simple recipe for bright, bitter, and healthful bitters, easily made and enjoyed in many a cocktail.

## Homemade Aromatic Bitters

*By Nick Kosevich, courtesy of Mortar & Pestle*

2 cups/480 ml high-proof American whiskey

2 cups/480 ml overproof rum

2 Tbsp gentian root

Two 6-in/15-cm cinnamon sticks

1 Tbsp green cardamom pods

1 Tbsp caraway seeds

1 Tbsp peeled and grated fresh ginger

1 jasmine tea bag

1 whole nutmeg, crushed

2 tsp coriander seeds

2 tsp black peppercorns

1 tsp ground allspice

1 tsp whole cloves

1 star anise pod

2 bay leaves

½ cup/85 g California raisins

Peel of 1 lemon in long strip

Peel of 1 orange in long strip

Peel of 1 lime in long strip

¼ tsp sea salt

2½ cups/600 ml hot water

¾ cup/150 g firmly packed light or dark brown sugar

¼ cup/60 ml honey

Combine the whiskey, rum, gentian, cinnamon, cardamom, caraway, ginger, tea bag, nutmeg, coriander seeds, peppercorns, allspice, cloves, star anise, bay leaves, raisins, citrus peels, and salt in a large glass jar with a sealable lid, cap tightly, and shake vigorously. Rest the jar on a kitchen shelf at room temperature for 21 days, shaking it once vigorously every day.

Line a fine-mesh sieve with cheesecloth and strain the contents of the jar through the sieve into a clean bowl, pressing and then squeezing the solids to release as much liquid as possible. Set the liquid—now the high-proof bitters base—aside. Transfer the solid mash to a saucepan, add the water, and place over low heat. Bring to a simmer and simmer for 15 minutes.

Remove from the heat, strain through the fine-mesh sieve into a bowl, and discard the solids. Add the brown sugar and honey to the warm liquid, stir to dissolve the sugar, and let cool completely.

Combine the cooled liquid and high-proof bitters base in a clean glass jar with a sealable lid, cap tightly, and shake vigorously. Return the jar to shelf for 7 days, shaking it once vigorously every day. Then leave the jar undisturbed for an additional week. Strain through a fine-mesh sieve lined with cheesecloth into a clean jar, then transfer to small bottles for cocktail use, leaving any sediment in the jar. Voila! The bitters are finally ready to use.

*Makes 3 small bottles of bitters.*

## Gentleman's Delight

*By Duggan McDonnell*

1½ oz/45 ml bianco (sweet white)
vermouth, such as Martini or Cinzano

¾ oz/25 ml dry gin

1 oz/30 ml fresh lemon juice

½ oz/15 ml Cocktail Syrup (page 59)

1 oz/30 ml tonic water

1 thin cucumber slice

6 dashes aromatic bitters, homemade
(see facing page) or store-bought

Pour the vermouth, gin, lemon juice, and
cocktail syrup into a mixing glass, add
ice, shake briefly, then strain into a large
punch glass filled with ice while simultaneously pouring in the tonic water. Garnish
with the cucumber slice, which is then
doused with the bitters.

# ON WHISKEY

America has had a love affair with whiskey since the colonial era, with George Washington building his own distillery in 1797. The United States is a land of many golden valleys, and whiskey making began as a very personal, local spirit. The whiskey in Pennsylvania was different from the whiskey in Virginia or Carolina and certainly different from what was found down in Kentucky and Tennessee. The source of grain was different, the actual pot still and stylistic preferences it could yield were different, and the branch—or river—water used to produce it and to cut the moonshine to aging and, later, to bottling strength was also different.

According to local history, hundreds of distilleries were producing whiskey in California by the Gay Nineties. The word *bourbon* originated in the East, specifically in the state of Virginia, where Bourbon County was. (Today, Bourbon County, now much smaller, lies in the state of Kentucky.) But in those early days of San Francisco, before the Pacific Railroad Act of 1862 and the building of the transcontinental railroad, a bottle of bourbon was nowhere to be seen. Even when the rails

opened in the 1870s, whiskey that was produced in the East largely remained in the East.

Before the storied valleys of Napa, Sonoma, and even Lodi and Livermore were planted under vine, grain was grown in them, much of it rye. The local distilleries used local crops and shipped their finished barrels locally, as well. But that was where the quality control stopped.

In those days, whiskey was the lowest common denominator of spirit. When we read of saloons in the Wild West and of cowboys yelling for whiskey, they might as well have been hollering "Hooch! Booze! Just something alcoholic in my cup, now please!" Worse than moonshine, it was the precursor to bathtub gin. Because grain was so prevalent, whiskey became the ubiquitous, though not preferred, tipple of the American West. The connoisseurship of American whiskey didn't begin until the end of the nineteenth century. Before then, much of the whiskey available in the West was tainted by saloon keepers—cut with water, colored with prune juice, fortified with other spirits, infused with chiles or even gunpowder—to stretch the volume and ferocity of every barrel. Unfortunately, because the public had not developed a palate for finer whiskey, many saloon keepers were quick to take advantage. But then came "Cocktail Bill" Boothby, who fell in love with, and then sought to incorporate, true, better whiskey into his cocktails.

These days, American whiskey has never tasted better. The renaissance in craft whiskey, and thus the renaissance in whiskey drinking in the United States, can be directly traced to San Francisco and Fritz Maytag of Anchor Brewers and Distillers. On December 9, 1994, the fine folks at Anchor, led by Maytag, filled their first barrel of 100 percent rye whiskey. It was something revolutionary, as rye wasn't popular in those days, and not a single rye whiskey produced in the United States was 100 percent rye. Twenty years later, America is in the midst of a boom in rye, bourbon, and craft whiskeys; and San Francisco, ever the innovative capital, led the way.

Interior of the Ideal Bar at 232 California Street, 1903

# SUPERIOR COCKTAIL WHISKEY

Cocktail whiskey should be a simple thing: absolutely delicious. It should be spicy, round, robust, and yet balanced. It should be a blend of different barrel treatments and a distillation of different grains, so as to arrive at the greatest complexity, and it should be easy on the palate but not too easy. After all, this isn't a sipping whiskey we're building here. This is a whiskey that will be shaken and stirred aplenty.

For this blend, I begin with Wild Turkey, a very strong and notorious rye whiskey that features both great spice and perceived alcohol content. This esteemed working-man's whiskey is the anchor of the blend. The counterpoint to such a rye is any of the sweeter, heavy-toasted sour mash whiskeys from Tennessee, such as George Dickel, Evan Williams, or the famed Jack Daniel's. On its own, young Tennessee whiskey can be a bit cloying; here, however, it adds the proper sweetness and depth. To finish the blend, I recommend employing Elijah Craig's 12-year-old bourbon. Not only is this bottle of bourbon fantastic but it's also highly underrated, and, like Buffalo Trace, it is one of the best values on the market. Also extremely elegant and subtle, it holds notes of chocolate and leather and tobacco that add layers to the more robust selections by Wild Turkey and the Tennessee whiskey.

As mentioned previously, when creating any blend of distilled spirits, time needs to be on your side. Unlike a cocktail, which is made quickly, involves ice and, thus, instant dilution, the blending of distilled spirits involves agitation (stirring) and aeration (pouring across from bucket to bucket). Only then, with additional time, will a magical balance be found.

## The Bartender's Secret Formula: Superior Cocktail Whiskey

17½ oz/500 ml Wild Turkey 81 rye

10½ oz/300 ml Tennessee sour mash

7 oz/200 ml Elijah Craig 12-year-old bourbon

Blend the liquid into a large vessel, such as a 1-gal/3.8-L pitcher, then allow to rest for 2 weeks before using.

*Makes 1 qt/1 L*

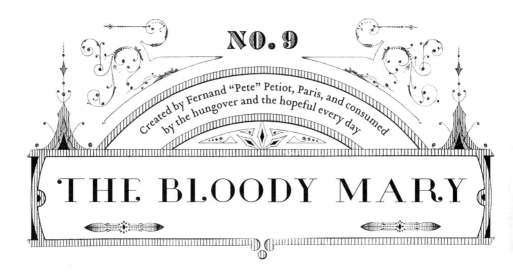

Created by Fernand "Pete" Petiot, Paris, and consumed by the hungover and the hopeful every day

# THE BLOODY MARY

## BLOODY MARY

1 Tbsp freshly grated horseradish

3 oz/90 ml tomato juice

2 oz/60 ml Square One organic vodka

2 oz/60 ml beef tea (see page 114)

½ oz/15 ml aquavit

½ oz/15 ml Dirty Sue olive juice

½ oz/15 ml fresh lemon juice

1 tsp Old Bay seasoning

1 tsp ground black pepper

1 tsp celery salt

2 dashes Worcestershire sauce

2 dashes hot sauce

Pickled vegetables, olives, citrus wheels, and fresh herbs for garnish

Muddle the horseradish in a mixing glass, then pour in the liquid and add the
Old Bay, pepper, celery salt, Worcestershire, and hot sauce.
Fill with ice, shake vigorously, then strain into a tall glass filled
with ice and garnish as desired.

The role of the Bloody Mary in San Francisco isn't so much that the drink was created here or that it is especially attuned to local taste preferences. Rather, it has to do with the City's history of day-time drinking. Unlike many states, California has no qualms about serving distilled spirits early in the morning. Strong drink has been available with the first meal of the day in California since before the state was part of the Union, even before the territory was part of Mexico. When Alta California was still a distant outpost of Spain, *vino* and aguardiente were already being enjoyed with *desayuno*. During the time I tended bar at San Francisco's most notorious and culinary brunch outpost, Absinthe Brasserie & Bar, I stirred plenty of heavily poured Sazeracs to pair with bacon and eggs before the noon hour. Flavorful liquid intoxicants are a wonderful accompaniment to any meal, and, of course, the standard drink nowadays to begin a morning (after) is the Bloody Mary.

The origins of this potent elixir are to be found in the Parisian bar with which San Franciscans hold much affinity: Harry's New York Bar, Sank Roo Doe Noo, Paris. Harry MacElhone and his crew of talented barmen created many masterpieces, several of which are dear to San Franciscans' hearts. The impressive list includes the Bloody Mary, first slung by barman Pete Petiot.

A Bloody Mary is thought to be the ultimate shim, the drink that will set you straight after a night that has left you feeling less than your best. It is the combination of pepper and acid and alcohol that seizes the palate and warms the blood, making the Bloody Mary a rousing success. We've all seen, if not experienced, white-knuckled quivering hands grasping for a breakfast menu and then the words *Bloody Mary* are overheard. Everything heightens the already painful headache. You know you need coffee, but all that the coffee will do is turn up the volume on the throbbing inside your head. The Bloody Mary, in contrast, will straighten out the curves in the road even when you're sitting still inside a breakfast diner.

The first sip is a painful attack, but then the tongue, swollen and dehydrated, abides, and halfway through the drink a light breaks through the fog. Bacon, ham, sausage, eggs, and more arrive. So too do a few more Bloody Marys. And then before the meal is finished and the check comes, the painful arrival has been forgotten and the day is set right toward good cheer. That's the lore of the Bloody Mary.

How do you like your Bloody Mary? With fresh horseradish or many dashes of Tabasco? Freshly cracked peppercorns or muddled diced ginger? Lemon juice or lime juice? Vodka, gin, or aquavit? Interpretations of the wildly popular drink abound, and passionately so.

The fine folks at Lefty O'Doul's restaurant in downtown San Francisco felt so strongly that their Bloody Mary was the best on the planet that they began bottling a commercial mix that is now employed in the cocktail throughout the region. But their claim of superiority has plenty of competitors, and nowadays anyone in a conversation about the quintessential San Francisco Bloody Mary would be remiss not to mention Zuni Café or Original Joe's. To sit curbside at Zuni on Market Street with two dozen oysters and a few Bloody Marys is widely regarded as the true San Francisco treat.

Across town in the bar of Original Joe's in North Beach, where the din of laughter is always a force to contend with, honest and ribald barkeeps conduct the chorus of the crowd. Behind-the-stick on a Saturday morning you might find Mike Fraser, with whom I share a passionate certainty about the Bloody Mary: it must include beef tea. Adding this restorative to the morning's shim magnifies its already high qualities, providing both real and liquid courage to the imbiber.

From time to time, I'll hop astride a bar stool in front of Mike, slide a little jar of beef tea across the wood, and let him do his magic. You see, Mike has been tending bar for more than four decades—no one needs to give the man direction. Only a minute later, he presents a perfect Bloody Mary, alight with peppered heat but not palate numbing. The best Bloody Mary also serves to stimulate the palate, to prep one for the forthcoming meal. Quickly then (which is how I finish every cocktail made by Mike), I'm feeling restored and ready for my breakfast, brunch, call it a very early dinner. My meal is about to arrive, and no matter what time this old barkeep chooses to begin his day, the Bloody Mary puts a little more gas in the proverbial tank.

# MAKE YOUR OWN BEEF TEA

8 oz/225 g lean organic beef, diced into small pieces

3 cups/720 ml water

1 carrot, peeled and diced

1 turnip, peeled and diced

1 cipollini onion, diced

1 celery stalk, diced

5 black peppercorns

½ tsp ground nutmeg

½ tsp salt

Combine the beef, water, vegetables, peppercorns, nutmeg, and salt in a wide-mouthed heat-resistant jar with a sealable lid and cap tightly. Place the jar in a saucepan and add water to the pan to reach two-thirds of the way up the side of the jar. Bring the water to a boil, turn the heat to the lowest setting, and simmer for 2 hours, adding hot water to the saucepan as needed to maintain the original level.

Remove the jar from the saucepan, let cool until it can be handled, and then remove the lid. Stir the contents to mix thoroughly, then pour through a fine-mesh sieve into a clean jar and discard the solids. Let cool, cover, and refrigerate for up to 3 weeks.

*Makes 3 cups/720 ml*

*Bartender standing in unidentified bar, n.d.*

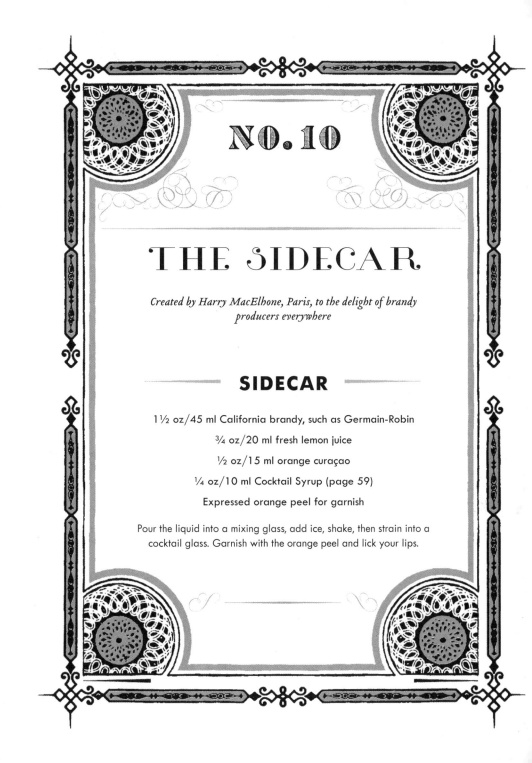

# THE SIDECAR

*Created by Harry MacElhone, Paris, to the delight of brandy producers everywhere*

## SIDECAR

1½ oz/45 ml California brandy, such as Germain-Robin

¾ oz/20 ml fresh lemon juice

½ oz/15 ml orange curaçao

¼ oz/10 ml Cocktail Syrup (page 59)

Expressed orange peel for garnish

Pour the liquid into a mixing glass, add ice, shake, then strain into a cocktail glass. Garnish with the orange peel and lick your lips.

To imagine a thriving vineyard inside San Francisco's city limits takes a lot of imagination. The City's often cold, foggy, breezy weather is nothing like that of the sunbaked Napa Valley ninety minutes to the northeast, where vineyards thrive. Grapes demand sunlight and heat and prefer a long, consistent growing season. San Francisco is clearly far from ideal.

Yet shortly after the Spanish settled in and began building the Misión San Francisco de Asís (now commonly called Mission Dolores), vineyards were planted. Exactly where those vines were cultivated, we no longer know. But sitting on the front steps of the mission near the corner of Sixteenth and Dolores Streets, one can imagine the old Hayes and Mission Creeks that flowed southeast toward Bernal Heights made this little valley great for agriculture. Then again, much of the surrounding landscape was covered in rolling hills of sand.

The vineyards likely didn't last a generation and were left fallow, as the Franciscan padres concentrated their efforts on other matters, leaving grape growing to the mission in Santa Clara and to those farther south. By the early 1800s, the vineyards of Los Angeles were highly successful, as were the plantings farther north in the great valley above Santa Barbara, near Mission San Gabriel Arcángel. It was brandy from these vines that made its way north to the Spanish military settlement known as the Presidio, to the mission, and then into the village of Yerba Buena. Today, California's great Central Valley is known as America's Brandyland.

These same territories also produced a massive amount of citrus, specifically lemons and oranges. Imagine then a cocktail with brandy (aguardiente de vino, as it was known then), lemon, and orange: Aha, the sidecar!

The modern narrative of the sidecar begins with Harry MacElhone in Paris and is a delightful combination of Cognac (French brandy), lemon, and Cointreau (a French orange liqueur and variation of curaçao.) It was invented during World War I, and a generation later, after World War II, many Americans knew of it and embraced the concoction Stateside. Whatever happened inside the walls of Harry's Bar, the whole of the world knew about it.

In the early nineteenth century, the Spanish citizens of California enjoyed their brandy in little punches, combinations of spirit, citrus, and sugar, sometimes dressed up a bit—much like the punches being enjoyed in Latin America in the same years. This mode of drinking was still common in San Francisco even after California became a state. In his esteemed 1882 tome, *New and Improved Bartender's Manual*, Harry Johnson includes a number of recipes for drinks remarkably similar to the sidecar, among them brandy sangaree, curaçao punch, and brandy punch. Plus, as noted earlier, the first decade after the gold rush saw the arrival in San Francisco of thousands of French citizens, many of them toting Cognac, Champagne, and other spirits that immediately influenced local drinking habits.

But the locally distilled brandy was the most widely consumed spirit in early San Francisco. Then, as now, brandy does wonders in cocktails, being so very mixable. In *California Brandy Drinks*, Malcolm R. Herbért writes, "There is no one correct taste, no one correct blend and no one correct brandy. One person's taste may favor a more full bodied brandy. Another person's taste likes a sweeter brandy and one person's might demand a full and pungent brandy. These variations of taste are based on closely guarded blends of the various brandymasters and that's what makes California brandy so exciting. There is brandy for almost every taste." And the cocktail most beloved by brandy drinkers is the sidecar.

\* \* \*

Years ago, after that first occasion with a Manhattan in Seattle and after I began to take cocktails seriously, I would visit bars that endeavored to serve proper cocktails and start every session by ordering a sidecar. The sidecar is the perfect cocktail to judge a barkeep's ability to arrive at balance. In its own unique way, it is a bold, bright marriage of alcohol, acid, and sugar. And it is balance that is the most important aspect of the sidecar, more so than any exactly written ratios for the recipe. Would I drink the sidecar if it was made with lime rather than lemon juice? Sure I would. Did I mind if a little cocktail syrup or perhaps a little moscato was used in place of the Cointreau? I didn't mind at all. In fact, that sort of innovation excites me! Was I pleased if a barkeep served me a sidecar and then shared that he had shaken it using California brandy? You bet I was. And what happened when a sidecar came across the wood that was not quite up to snuff? I would finish the cocktail completely but quietly and then move on to a glass of wine, or perhaps depart for another locale. The sidecar was my litmus test, the bellwether drink that determined whether the bartender would earn my trust as a craftsman.

For me—and for most San Franciscans—the sidecar is a bright, balanced import from Harry's New York Bar, Paris. It is dry and highly quaffable and boasts a style of cocktail construction that has been popular in California for more than two centuries. And although the early vineyards of Mission Dolores certainly failed beneath our fog-canopied summers, we have the same fog to thank for driving us into our saloons to enjoy the bounty of bottles.

## Cable Car

*By Tony Abou-Ganim, courtesy of the Starlight Room*

Lemon wedge and cinnamon sugar

1½ oz/45 ml spiced rum

½ oz/15 ml orange curaçao

1 oz/30 ml fresh lemon juice

½ oz/15 ml Cocktail Syrup (page 59)

Expressed orange peel for garnish

Dampen the rim of a cocktail glass with the lemon wedge, then coat with the cinnamon sugar. Pour the liquid into a mixing glass, add ice, shake, then fine-strain into the rimmed cocktail glass and garnish with the orange peel.

## Champs-Élysées

*A revived classic of disputed origin, shaken in San Francisco many years ago by Duggan McDonnell*

1½ oz/45 ml Armagnac

¾ oz/20 ml fresh lemon juice

½ oz/15 ml green Chartreuse

½ oz/15 ml Cocktail Syrup (page 59)

3 dashes aromatic bitters, homemade (see page 104) or store-bought

3 dashes orange curaçao

Expressed lemon peel for garnish

Pour the liquid into a mixing glass, add ice, shake, then fine-strain into a cocktail glass and garnish with the lemon peel.

## Vieux Carré

*An adaptation of a New Orleans classic, beloved by the barmen of Absinthe Brasserie & Bar*

1½ oz/45 ml California brandy

½ oz/15 ml rye whiskey

½ oz/15 ml Italian vermouth

¼ oz/10 ml Bénédictine D.O.M.

2 dashes Peychaud's bitters

2 dashes aromatic bitters, homemade (see page 104) or store-bought

Expressed lemon peel for garnish

Pour the liquid into a mixing glass, add ice, stir forty times, then strain into a rocks glass over a single stone of ice and garnish with the lemon peel.

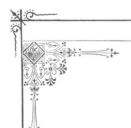

# CITRUS AND
# SAN FRANCISCO

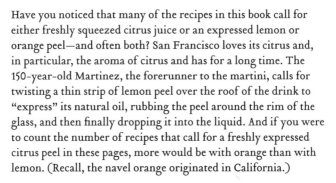

Have you noticed that many of the recipes in this book call for either freshly squeezed citrus juice or an expressed lemon or orange peel—and often both? San Francisco loves its citrus and, in particular, the aroma of citrus and has for a long time. The 150-year-old Martinez, the forerunner to the martini, calls for twisting a thin strip of lemon peel over the roof of the drink to "express" its natural oil, rubbing the peel around the rim of the glass, and then finally dropping it into the liquid. And if you were to count the number of recipes that call for a freshly expressed citrus peel in these pages, more would be with orange than with lemon. (Recall, the navel orange originated in California.)

Just what exactly does an expressed citrus peel do for a cocktail? It brightens the liquid, freshening the aroma and tightening the flavor molecules. It keeps a Martinez from seeming flabby, prevents a Manhattan from tasting overly boozy, and absolutely integrates a Negroni. In other words, the peel is an indispensable ingredient in each of these mighty classics.

The barman's best tool for fashioning a clean, precise peel for expressing over a cocktail is the old-fashioned potato peeler. Unlike the usual channel or paring knife, a potato peeler does not remove any bitter pith from the fruit, just a thin strip of skin that is easily twisted or pinched over the drink's surface to release a fine spray of oils into the delight below—a simple trick that makes a great cocktail better.

# ON BRANDY

Brandy, originally known as aguardiente de vino, was the first distilled spirit produced in California and, in the form of Pisco and Cognac, its most popular import. But it has fallen out of fashion as the cocktail set turned toward gin, tequila, and other spirits for inspiration. The Sazerac, the mint julep, and more began with brandy. Nowadays this once prized spirit is primarily relegated to fortifying sangria on both coasts and to mixing up the heartily consumed brandy old fashioned in the middle of the country. But this need not be the case.

The noble grape spirit can be mixed mightily in many cocktails, such as that original Parisian beauty, the sidecar, or its evolved cousin, the Champs-Élysées, or the Vieux Carré of French New Orleans. It can also be resurrected in many fresh, improvised drinks. It is my hope, and my prediction, that one day soon the first spirit of California will experience a renaissance.

# SUPERIOR COCKTAIL BRANDY

After tasting your own batch of cocktail brandy, you will surely agree with me that brandy is due for a renaissance. The base for this blend should be a brandy that the palate of the general consumer is both familiar and comfortable with, so begin with a V.S. Cognac from Martell, Rémy Martin, or Pierre Ferrand. Cognac is doubly distilled, and the V.S. style is lighter, having been aged for only a few years. The layering for this blend is quite fun: the Pineau des Charentes contributes youthful grape taste and a brighter flavor profile along with lowered alcohol. This is counteracted by the Armagnac, which has higher alcohol and a leaner, single-distilled flavor profile. The Pisco, bottled from a single vineyard of Moscatel, contributes not only body but also bold aromas, and floral flavor, a quality that is compounded by the slightly saline, slightly sweet amontillado sherry, an addition that also stretches the mouthfeel and increases complexity.

After a thorough integration and resting period, this blend tastes familiar yet better than any one brandy on its own. Brandies always benefit from blending, from the symphony that many different eaux-de-vie offer when brought together. Here, the production style of each of the expressions varies significantly, but as they all are 100 percent grape based, they meld into one another effortlessly.

This, I confess, is my favorite Bartender's Secret Formula to blend, and all too often, at the end of the night, it comes out of the speed rail and a little glass is poured for yours truly.

## The Bartender's Secret Formula: Superior Cocktail Brandy

24½ oz/700 ml V.S. Cognac

3½ oz/100 ml Pineau des Charentes

3½ oz/100 ml Armagnac

1¾ oz/50 ml Campo de Encanto Dist. RSV Single Vine Moscatel

1¾ oz/50 ml amontillado sherry

Blend the liquid into a large vessel, such as a 1-gal/3.8 L pitcher, then allow to rest for 1 week before using.

*Makes 1 qt/1 L*

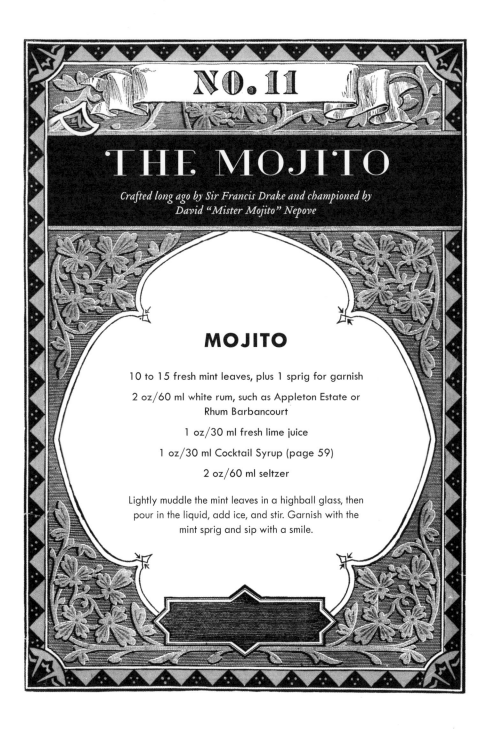

# THE MOJITO

*Crafted long ago by Sir Francis Drake and championed by*
*David "Mister Mojito" Nepove*

## MOJITO

10 to 15 fresh mint leaves, plus 1 sprig for garnish

2 oz/60 ml white rum, such as Appleton Estate or
Rhum Barbancourt

1 oz/30 ml fresh lime juice

1 oz/30 ml Cocktail Syrup (page 59)

2 oz/60 ml seltzer

Lightly muddle the mint leaves in a highball glass, then
pour in the liquid, add ice, and stir. Garnish with the
mint sprig and sip with a smile.

In 1996, David Nepove stepped behind-the-stick at Enrico's Sidewalk Café on Broadway and Mister Mojito was born. His self-proclaimed moniker was in line with his ancestors: Professor Jerry Thomas as Jupiter Olympus and "Cocktail Bill" Boothby as Presiding Deity at their respective bars. David's choice of title was clearly culinary minded and cocktail obsessed, and it came at a time—at the very beginning—when bartenders across the land refused to make mojitos for their customers. The bright and refreshing tipple from Havana was starting its ascent in popularity, and rather than acclimate to popular demand, thousands of cocktail programs simply refused to accept the preferences of popular culture. These bars did not stock fresh mint—or anything else—to muddle, nor did they dare to lightly layer rum, lime, sugar, and then seltzer atop the delicate mint to create a sublime highball.

Not so at Enrico's with David Nepove at the helm. Mister Mojito, like the barkeeps who came before him, separated himself from the herd of mediocrity by being willing to work just a little harder. (Admittedly, the sophomoric Long Island iced tea does call for two more ingredients than the mojito.) His salt-of-the-earth approach endeared him to many and became an undeniable influence on modern mixology—it was Mister Mojito who, in 1996, started the farm-to-glass mixology movement.

The idea of herbs or other fresh ingredients in cocktails was not new even then, however. As noted earlier, fresh mint, for example, has played a role in San Francisco cocktail programs since the gold rush days, when wild mint flourished in the area.

Mister Mojito and I share a passion for fresh cocktails, and the best ingredients for creating them are found at the Heart of the City Farmers' Market on Wednesday mornings in United Nations Plaza. There, along Market Street, with the golden dome of City Hall within view, local farmers set up shop to sell their produce.

To walk among the stalls lined with produce from Marin County, the Central Valley, and Watsonville right in the middle of the City, the ground lightly shaking from the BART and MUNI trains rumbling below, is an experience not to be missed. The market is invariably crowded with all kinds of shoppers, from neighborhood residents and workers to restaurateurs, chefs, and bar folks. Here it is easy to find California citrus, peppermint, and even lemon verbena, all of which will make a good mojito even better. Of course, using them requires a little extra work, but the philosophy that drove Mr. Mojito was a sound one: fresh ingredients and a spirit of innovation always deliver a delicious reward.

Nepove embraced the barkeep's best friend, the wooden pestle, and enthusiastically muddled every fresh fruit and herb available to deliver bright, balanced cocktails in an era when many patrons didn't seem to care.

The timing of Nepove's ascent and passion is critically important, too. It was just before the first dot-com boom in San Francisco, just before the first flood of dollars and persons and ideas arrived and changed the culture of the City. Fast-forward to 2002, after Silicon Valley had collapsed, the economy was going sideways, and San Francisco was wondering what its identity had become. Mister Mojito was still behind-the-stick, muddling kumquats and raspberries at Enrico's Sidewalk Café, but something was different in San Francisco. That brief era between 1996 and 2002 had permanently moved the City from its post–World War II identity as a blue-collar town into the globally recognized center of technological and culinary innovation it is today.

Although the rush of money and ideas had altered the City forever, one of the things that stuck was a tradition that reached back to the 1850s: fresh cocktails. In 1996, before the Internet was widespread and cell phones were ubiquitous, David Nepove likely felt that Enrico's was an island, alone in its passion for fresh mixology. But by 2002, nearly everyone was equipped with a cell phone, every urban neighborhood had at least one Internet café, and if you were a barman or just a cocktail connoisseur looking to taste delicious cocktails and absorb a bit of mixing philosophy, you walked beneath the neon lights of Broadway and there, on the old Barbary Coast, snuggled amid the strip clubs, you would find Enrico's.

At least, that's how I remember it.

## The Draquecito, or Sir Francis Drake's Mojito
*By Duggan McDonnell*

10 to 15 fresh mint leaves, plus 1 sprig for garnish

2 oz/60 ml Campo de Encanto Dist. RSV Single Vine Quebranta Pisco

1 oz/30 ml fresh lime juice

1 oz/30 ml Cocktail Syrup (page 59)

2 oz/60 ml seltzer

Lightly muddle the mint leaves in a highball glass, then pour in the liquid, add ice, and stir. Garnish with the mint sprig.

## Missionary's Downfall
*Adapted from Donn Beach*

10 to 15 fresh mint leaves, plus 1 sprig for garnish

1½ oz/45 ml white rum

¾ oz/20 ml fresh lime juice

¾ oz/20 ml pineapple juice

½ oz/15 ml brandy

½ oz/15 ml Cocktail Syrup (page 59)

3 dashes peach bitters

Lightly muddle the mint leaves in a highball glass, then pour in the liquid, add ice, and stir. Garnish with the mint sprig.

# THE ANCESTRY OF
# THE WORLD'S FIRST DRINK

The mojito is believed to be the world's oldest cocktail, but its paternity, despite what is commonly believed, isn't exactly Cuban.

There is widespread agreement in the Caribbean that the origin of the bright and refreshing highball known today as the mojito can be traced to the hands of El Draque, as Sir Francis Drake was known. Drake, whose name is eerily similar to "the Dragon" in Catalan, was mightily feared by the Spanish after pillaging many of her colonies. The mojito began as the Draquecito, and it was likely created during Drake's return to the West Indies in 1585, when the British privateer's confidence was high, when he drank freely of his enemy's nectar and flaunted his successes. For well over a decade, Drake, the world's first pirate of global renown, tormented the Spanish. During his first voyage and circumnavigation of the globe in 1579, he repeatedly sought to destroy and pillage Spanish settlements in the Caribbean, off the coast of Peru, in California, and then in the Philippines.

But in 1585, rum, the distilled spirit of sugarcane or molasses, did not exist, even though sugarcane, sugar, and the juice of the plant were in common use. So, Drake's Draquecito did not originate with rum.

The Spanish were regarded as the best winemakers and distillers of the era. In colonial Peru, where it had been but a little more than fifty years since Pizarro had founded the first Spanish settlement, excellent wine was being produced. Within just a generation the valley not far from the port of Pisco had become famous for vineyards, its little distilleries.

As noted earlier, Pizarro had sailed out of the Spanish port of Sanlúcar de Barrameda, Jerez, and now some five decades later, Pisco had much in common with Sanlúcar. The same grapes were being grown nearby, and wine making was handled in a similar fashion. Young red wine was produced, then a portion of it was quickly distilled and immediately added back to the young wine to fortify it for safekeeping. Throughout the region, this fortified wine and its aguardiente de vino were available and traded in Pisco.

In 1579, El Draque rounded the horn of South America and crept up the coast of Peru. There, in the little harbor of Pisco, he sacked the ships and then raided the town. He returned to his ships with many prisoners and demanded the finest aguardiente produced in the valley for their release. Drake was allegedly given three hundred *botijas* (large clay amphorae) in exchange for the captured Pisqueros, and his promise to sail away quickly.

Weeks later, El Draque and his fleet sailed into the bay just north of San Francisco now named after him. The captain and his men went ashore, where they rested for six weeks in a landscape covered with wild mint. During that time, with both mint and Pisco plentiful, Drake and his merry men likely fashioned the earliest form of the mojito. You see, both sugarcane (as sweetener) and limes were available throughout the Caribbean and along the Spanish territories of the Pacific, so Drake undoubtedly acquired those in his raids, as well.

Six years later, in 1585, after having presented his many treasures, including both Pisco and the potato, to the British crown, Drake returned to Cuba, and in the hull of his ship, we imagine that he carried a few botijas of *aguardiente de Pisco*. (In Cuba, before the word *rum* came into being, the distillate was known as *aguardiente de caña*. This was the first use of the term *aguardiente* for a distilled spirit produced from something other than grapes. Hence, the confusion and assumption that the mojito originated with rum.) Drake returned to the Caribbean and took with him his favorite tipple, which became known as the Draquecito, a bright concoction inspired by his first voyage around the world, his time in California, his hatred of Spain, and his passion for drinking his enemy's nectar.

# THE FARMERS' MARKET IN
# THE COCKTAIL GLASS

On Wednesday mornings, I shop at the Heart of the City Farmers' Market, and on Saturdays, I stroll along the waterfront at the Ferry Plaza Building, sniffing, squeezing, picking at the many fruits and vegetables on vibrant display. Both venues are fantastic markets and both attract barmen and chefs from the City's top restaurants. In addition to fresh herbs and the best eggs year-round, I hunt for specialty citrus and berries. If I am not tending bar that night, I make certain that the barkeeps on duty understand that their toy chest, their arsenal, has a few new things in it for the evening. When blood oranges are fantastic at the end of autumn, I'll slice a bowlful of them in half and set them atop the bar, ready for juicing.

Shopping at a farmers' market for fresh produce ensures two things: the quality and the variety of the ingredients will be unmatched. You won't find large Mexican sweet limes or five types of basil at your conventional supermarket. Farmers' markets provide the inspiration that puts new flavors into the contemporary cocktails of San Francisco.

Considerable attention has been paid to the resurgence of interest in the fresh cocktail brought about by the link between the farmers' market and the bar, and rightfully so. Not many local bartenders were shopping for different varieties of mint in farmers' markets in the 1970s and 1980s. With the advent of the twenty-first century and the money to match, the City's bartenders began seeking out the best and freshest ingredients. Then again, this is all highly reminiscent of the gold rush and Comstock Lode eras, when disposable incomes were incredibly high and the imagination of the bartender aimed to please.

Also, without the farmers' markets, the wooden pestle, or barkeep's muddler, would not have come back into common use. It wasn't just the mojito and the Ginger Rogers being muddled around San Francisco in the old days. Plenty of other fresh, fruit-forward cocktails were being mixed up, too. The bounty of California has always been shipped to and sold in San Francisco, from the early days when fresh berries, mint, and much more were at the barkeep's elbow. In San Francisco, the farm has long been in the glass.

*Man standing behind the bar of Warner's Cobweb Palace, Meigg's Wharf, n.d.*

# 1,001 NIGHTS BEHIND BARS

*Nel mezzo del cammin di nostra vita,*
*mi ritrovai per una selva oscura,*
*ché la diritta via era smarrita.*

—DANTE, *The Divine Comedy*

Midway through life,
there I was, in a dark wood,
lost, with no road to follow.

It was the summer of 2002, when I was in the middle of a quickie divorce from a quicker marriage begun at too young an age. I earned but a few hundred bucks a week as a lackluster bar back. Most of that came via kickbacks from waitresses whose cups I'd refill with Stoli vanilla and Diet Coke, in between schlepping beer glasses and changing kegs. And then in the rain- and stench-soaked alley behind downtown Seattle's Wild Ginger restaurant, I never knew how many empty Merlot bottles I would have to pitch to make all those rats darting at my boots scatter.

My home was a one-room shack perched at the end of a dock on beautiful Lake Sammamish, about thirty minutes east of downtown Seattle. I had moved out the boating gear and the previous tenants: spiders and rodents who'd occupied the eight-by-ten-foot abode. In came my bed and books. Rent was three hundred dollars a month. Every morning, I'd walk above the water and ponder what may come next. I thought I was Thoreau and Sammamish was my would-be Walden. Some days I felt a new, rising confidence. Most, I didn't.

I'd come home after a hard day's work that I couldn't resent, a work for which, for some reason, I had talent and was paid to perform. On sunny mornings, I'd look out over the water and not know what the day would bring, and then in the dark night so full of stars because Seattle was many miles west, I'd fear going to sleep. I dreaded waking to yet another day without purpose, without any direction.

I was vexed, depressed, and insecure as all hell that summer of 2002.

What skill set I may have had, I was unaware of at the time. My bachelor's degree seemed of little practical use, and I couldn't produce anything on paper worth publishing. I was a part-time drunk, a charmer, a boy-man nearing thirty years of age with few calluses on his hands. I'd passed judgment on myself: I couldn't work worth a damn. I was but a lowly bar back, and on one of those mornings looking out over the lake with the first scent of autumn in the air, I hatched a desperate notion—I needed to rebrand myself. I needed to move, and then move up to become a real barman.

I returned home to California, to San Francisco, the city of my forefathers, and, like them, I would attempt to make myself a life. So, after arriving in Fog City, I did what many other bartenders have done. I turned my résumé into a piece of fiction.

With years of experience listed on that résumé, I landed at MECCA in the City's Castro district, near the end of its reign as one of San Francisco's fabulous high-volume hotspots. Behind the bar was a machine that made frozen Bellinis, the oft-derided cordial Sour Apple Pucker lived in the speed rail, and the word *cosmo* was squealed across the bar more times than I cared to count. It must have been obvious to all that I hadn't mastered the kinetic aspect of tending bar, using my right hand to pour the liquid into the mixing glass, using my left hand to scoop the ice into the glass, and then using both hands to shake and flip the concoction, slapping off the shaker and straining the new and magical liquid into the cocktail glass—all in the matter of a few, beautiful seconds. I couldn't do any of it . . . yet. That was evident to the bar manager, Paul D'Agostino, too. But Paul hadn't hired me; Carl Christiansen, one of the delightful owners, had. And Carl liked me. Although when it was only Paul and me working together behind-the-stick, Paul refused to speak to me. Not a word.

"I've got a strip steak and a roast chicken for Bar 11 and 12. Who's having what?" I'd ask Paul while holding hot plates of food in my hands.

Nothing.

"Didn't you fire the order? Do you remember what each guest ordered?"

Crickets.

My favorite shift of the week at MECCA was Sunday afternoon. There was a drag show and hundreds of the Castro's finest slammed the bar immediately after pumping iron at their respective gyms, donning oh-so-flattering tees and jeans, and then oozing themselves all over one another and MECCA's zinc bar top. It never failed to be *a fucking busy* shift. I loved working those Sundays, open to close, slamming out lemon drops and vodka tonics and the occasional shot of tequila, and laughing at the female impersonators with the boys, all the way to the bank.

*   *   *

The night that changed my life, the shift that consecrated Duggan McDonnell a barman, was New Year's Eve, December 31, 2002. Just a few months after the smell of change had filled the autumn air, I was scheduled as the last bartender to arrive, knowing I would have to work the service well for the busiest night of the year. By nine o'clock, with the second dinner seating about to begin, I was starting to drown in drink tickets. I was, as the saying goes, in the weeds. Every course was paired with a different glass of wine. Cordials and Cognac were being ordered as after-dinner drinks, and then at ten o'clock, the front door was opened to the public and all of Market Street swarmed inside.

MECCA's service well was located at the bottom end of its long oval bar, which faced both the kitchen and about fifty square feet of unseated concrete that would become the dance floor. It was the only available space for people to gather. And can you guess to which bartender all immediately flocked? At any given moment, twelve drink tickets printed noisily out in front of me, while a horde of men and women glowing with the excitement of the coming year stood, stared, and (because it was MECCA) slowly mouthed their drink orders at me, running their tongue over their top lip and then gleefully snapping their fingers at me.

"Holy fuck!" I shouted to myself. "I am busy! And I am doing a shit, horrible, stuck-in-the-weeds job here. And will these queens please find another barkeep to pick on for five minutes!"

The night, the pain necessitated change; I needed to take control of my little world. Orders for glasses of wine were poured along the left side of the tiny square of bar top belonging to me. Shots and spirits poured neat were placed horizontally along the front, and as the vast need was for cocktails, larger and varied glassware took up most of the workspace in front of me. If I had drink tickets that contained three lemon drops with one Cosmopolitan, I'd make four lemon drops and then splash cranberry juice into one and call it the Cosmo. If there were sidecars and margaritas, I'd shake the modifying ingredients together (lime, Cointreau, and so on), then strain each one into the respective glass while simultaneously pouring in the shot of brandy and of tequila.

The night blew to just before midnight; my hands ached, literally frozen by the constant shaking of ice inside metal tins, of grasping the metal ice scoop and those cold Boston shakers hour after hour. I looked up and witnessed waitresses frantically passing out glasses of paltry Prosecco in preparation for the midnight toast. Their faces were filled with resentment; this gesture from the house took them away from their tables, and the crowd wasn't tipping them. Nor did the crowd want the bubbles. They wanted the handsome barmen to sling them more and more cocktails. And so it was that the final countdown came: ten, nine, eight, seven—and I was frantically shaking and sending out cocktails, spinning bottles, flipping tins and glassware. I was moving like I'd never moved before: fast, strong, precise. Sweat dropped into the ice below, smiles turned to scowls and back to smiles again before my eyes as the throng had to wait for their reward. None of that mattered—at least not to me. I was working harder than I had ever worked before, and I was loving it. I was the one working for all of them, and I wanted, demanded that they order more cocktails, spend more money, laugh and kiss and cry, and then to do it all over again. I was the one who had entered the New Year with a goddamn purpose.

At the end of the shift, I hobbled across the street into the Safeway where there was an ATM. I needed to immediately deposit the cash tips I'd earned. I was broke, it was the first of the month, and the rent was due. It was nearly five in the morning, and there, sticking out of the cash machine waiting for me, was four hundred dollars.

Ah, but 2003 would be a wonderful year!

* * *

A few months later, I picked up a single shift at ThirstyBear Brewing Company, which held massive parties on Saturday nights and needed an extra gunslinger. The taciturn bar manager was Daniel Shoemaker, and although good-humored, he was all business. This is the same Daniel who, a few years later, migrated north to Portland, Oregon, and then led the cocktail revolution in the Rose City with the opening of his Teardrop Lounge. At ThirstyBear, I learned how to make an Incredible Hulk, a cocktail composed of equal parts Hpnotiq and Cognac. (The French must have been so proud!) And the thousands who flocked to these parties shouted out their favorite cocktails across the wood to Daniel and me, "Midori sour!" "Surfer on acid!" "Adios motherfucker!"

Those steam-filled nights of chaos were either feast or famine when it came to the level of business the promoter could deliver. And between bouts of racing to see who could pour more, who could "ring" more dollars into the cash register, Daniel and I would toast each other with buckets of beer: old fashioned glasses that we'd fill with lager and empty down our gullets in two seconds. The bartending style was extremely physical, yet beyond all that, Daniel and I came to regard each other as culinary curiosities, as a pair of intellects more interested in tasting Rioja, discussing restaurant reviews, and dissecting James Joyce than in slinging Strong Island iced tea to the masses.

The time came, and I had to leave MECCA. The level of business had dropped. The sense of community had moved on. Paul was there. I sought out a position in a bar with a steep and storied reputation for cocktails in San Francisco, where Tony Abou-Ganim had set the standard before being plucked to open the Bellagio in Las Vegas, where Marco Dionysos now held forth. I found myself sitting across from Harry Denton interviewing for a gig in his Starlight Room.

"How would you like it if I gave you a blow job?" Harry asked, with a wicked smile.

"Some other time," I said, hardly frazzled.

Our dialogue was a light pitter-patter, interjecting business with bits of San Francisco repartee. "What do you want to be doing in five years?" he asked me, now earnest.

"I'll be running my own bar," I answered, saying it aloud for the first time. To me, it sounded like practice, like a little lie, as though I should have rehearsed it before meeting with Harry.

"Good," he answered. "And you will. Work for me. Work in this corporate ladder. Learn from it and make as many mistakes using other peoples' money as you can."

(Was this really happening? I asked myself. In an interview?)

Four years later, just one block from where Harry and I first met, I opened Cantina in May 2007.

* * *

Those four years were like dog years. I tended bar and traveled the world; I wrote wine lists and visited distilleries; I amassed a huge collection of books on food, wine, spirits, and cocktails; and I won cocktail competitions. I cofounded San Francisco Cocktail Week. I drank like a fish, falling head over heels in love with amaro, mezcal, and tequila, with Pisco and fortified wines, and I dined at some of the best restaurants in the country. Then, brands hired me for my opinion, my expertise, my hard-earned consultancy. And, of course, there was that feature in *Food & Wine* magazine.

A turning point in San Francisco's cocktail culture came in 2006, while I was tending bar at Absinthe Brasserie & Bar. The change was particularly evident during the Sunday brunch shift, when the waiters would deliver a barrage of cocktail orders before noon: Pimm's cup! Ramos gin fizz! Bellini! Bloody Mary! Sazerac! In just a few years, a world that had been flat, chugging the Incredible Hulk, had become a new, round world of Sazeracs lightly stirred, then swilled alongside plates of eggs and bacon. The *San Francisco Chronicle*'s wine section led by Jon Bonné began featuring regular coverage of cocktails and spirits, pointing readers toward restaurants with real talent behind their bars. A profound cocktail renaissance had arrived.

These days, the San Francisco Bay Area is home to an absolute plethora of talent. Mixologists, bar chefs, cocktailians—all are nomenclature for a motley crew, including me. The culture has wholeheartedly returned to its roots as a drinking town, a bastion of culinary tourism, where drinking a cocktail is as de rigueur as riding a cable car.

"The massively important milestone in the cocktail movement was when *Food & Wine* magazine declared 2006 to be the Year of the Cocktail," Gaz Regan, author of *The Joy of Mixology* and contributor to the *San Francisco Chronicle*, said to me. "Now an authority comes along and says to the foodies, cocktails are legitimate." I know, Gaz, I thought to myself, I know, because I was in that issue. I was one of the bartenders featured as a leader of the American cocktail revolution. One night, shortly after that issue of *Food & Wine* hit the newsstands, I was tending bar at frisson, the ne'er-do-well short-lived hotspot on Jackson Street. As usual, I was hammering away at drink tickets in the well, when all of a sudden a woman standing before me hoisted the magazine toward me.

"Can I have an autograph?" she asked.

My jaw dropped, a single sweat bead pitched from my forehead into the margarita I'd just made, and a cocktail server, waiting for his glass of Barolo, impatiently tapped his finger on the bar top. But the woman's smile was sincere, sweet. And she was waiting. "What's your name?" I asked, removing the permanent marker from her hand.

There have been television shows focused on cocktails, on bartenders. I have been filmed for a few, too. The issue of "celebrity" has come up, and rightfully so. And not just for me, please understand. I'm not the only one whose history goes from broke and insecure to talented and thriving. In his heyday as a San Francisco bartender, Jerry Thomas was said to have earned more money than the vice president of the United States. Trader Vic became a household name—and stayed one for generations—because his cocktail style was so unique and so damn good. Plenty of talented Bay Area bar folks are living a similar life today.

At Cantina over the years, many folks have come in and asked for me by name—people from Melbourne and New York, Los Angeles and Seattle. The Internet is available to everyone, even on our cell phones. These cocktail tourists, these nomadic spirit geeks are rabid for their next imbibing pleasure, having done an excellent job of researching venues and the talent behind them.

I've been thinking more and more about all of this, about what importance a bar, a bartender, a cocktail can play in a person's life. On a recent Saturday, after I closed the bar, I sat there on a lumpy bar stool and reflected on what has happened in the past ten years in San Francisco and on the many, many thousands of lives I've touched. I'd returned earlier in the week from Peru, where I'd spent a week traveling, followed by time blending tanks of single-vineyard, single-varietal Pisco for my beloved brand, Encanto, and then flying overnight through multiple airports back home to the City. I was exhausted, and on that particular night, I had spent fourteen hours on my feet. And so I sat and looked around the place, first at the back bar full of bottles, several hundred strong. All of the lights were up, too bright; the saccharine scent of crushed citrus and burnt wax was in the air; and broken glass, matches, and mint were underfoot. Toby Cecchini writes in his barman's memoir, *Cosmopolitan: A Bartender's Life*, "There is an ephemeral hour then when the bar, like a woman *d'un certain âge*, cleverly cloaked in evening light to conceal flaws she knows are beneath consideration, glows with an imperfect, hard-used loveliness." This was not that hour. Cantina had performed well, but now both of us were beyond tired. I felt like a ballerina after having danced a matinee of *The Nutcracker*, soaking her corns in a tub of salt and tears. And the aroma in the bar? Like the bright stink of the Barbary Coast at sunrise.

\* \* \*

"Most people who come in here have no idea what we do behind the bar," Tony Abou-Ganim said to me one day while we sipped Negronis in Cantina. Tony is the Joe DiMaggio of cocktails, a middle-class kid with a great smile and a humble heart who's come up because he's got talent. To look at Tony is to recognize guts. His build is that of a classic prizefighter, his gaze direct. I asked him what the most critical factor is to continuing his work—post–Bellagio, Las Vegas, post–large consulting contracts with global spirits conglomerates. He replied, "The brand." That is, the brand of Tony.

And that is exactly what celebrity bartenders and the infamous bars that birthed them have always been: brands. Harry Johnson, in the introduction to his 1882 book, trumpeted "In presenting this Manual to the public, I beg the indulgence for making a few remarks in regard to myself having been in the Hotel and Saloon business, in various capacities since my boyhood, studying and practising the tastes and fancies of the public in regard to drinking, and having travelled all over this and other countries, I have after careful preparation, time and expense, compiled this work, which I challenge any party to criticize against or find one receipt which is not fully and completely prepared. I have been employed in some of the most prominent, leading and first class Hotels and Saloons in this city as well as all other parts of the United States and other countries, from which I have the very highest letters of recommendation, as to my complete knowledge of managing a Saloon, and preparing drinks of every kind and form." Johnson, it seems, had much to rail against. Or was it that he simply had the persona of a great barman, that like many other self-made entrepreneurs he understood the need to promote and then protect one's worth?

Gaz Regan, ever the salty stalwart of American cocktail culture, relayed, "You don't open a shoe shop and not tell anyone about it!" Which I take to mean, you would be stupid not to promote the quality of your work. For many years now, most San Franciscans have been under the impression that Duncan Nicol invented the Pisco punch at the Bank Exchange Saloon. He didn't. Nicol wasn't even born when the joint opened. Rather, after immigrating to the United States, he worked his way up in the business and then perfected and marketed the Pisco punch best. Plus, he marketed his saloon along with it better than anyone in the West during his era, which made both Nicol and his Pisco punch famous.

It has been more than ten years since I began my own branding effort by crafting that fictional résumé, attempting to make myself into a barman. I sat on that lumpy bar stool after a long shift and I was tired, the lights were all up, and I wondered how these seemingly disparate factors of work and play and drink and branding all come together in a meaningful way. But more than that, I was thinking about all the people who have crossed my path during those countless moments of shaking, serving, and sharing cocktails. I met my wife, Felicia, inside Cantina; my business partners, Aaron and Christine, were married in the bar; and many wedding receptions, first dates, and other liaisons have happened within its four walls. I could not count them all. The memories warmed me. Had I found that sense of purpose I had begun searching for ten years ago?

Toby Cecchini published his memoir in 2003, the same year I became a proper barman and enjoyed that curious interview with Harry Denton. Cecchini's star had risen quickly in Manhattan's bar circles after his stint at the Odeon and then opening Passerby in Chelsea. But it wasn't until *Cosmopolitan* was released that bartenders and cocktail geeks across the globe knew his name. "Suddenly, I was that bartender guy who writes about drinks," Toby told me. For a time, Toby was the brightest star in bartending. "I've always made great drinks. But, the Passerby [was] the antithesis of that. I liked the mice and the cockroaches. I like running a bar's bar." I dig what you're saying, Toby. I really do.

Like Toby, like many before me, I have toiled and then sat alone at the end of a shift in the glare of the postcocktail light, three fingers of spirit in one hand. The memory of filling glasses half full with Stoli vanilla, then layering in a splash of Diet Coke and a few ice cubes hour after hour for an extra twenty bucks remains fresh in my mind. It was just yesterday that I was that young, insecure bar back, the lackey made to sprint up and down flights of stairs with cases of whiskey atop my shoulders, to stoop into walk-in coolers to change heavy kegs of beer, to scorch blood-cut fingers squeezing limes, all the while being pranked by the bartenders. They'd quietly drop a whole egg into my pants pocket and then deftly smack it, saying, "Good job, kid!" I can still feel the oozing yolk and brittle shell on my hand hours later, as I would reach in to find my keys. Those bartenders, elder and wiser than me, fooled me night after night, until that New Year's Eve came when this saloon keeper fell in love with work—true callous-forming work. That single night when I became a barman.

At any point in life, we may wonder which road to follow. As a saloon owner, I can attest to having seen this across the bar and hearing it from my guests more than a few times. Bars see many moments of people questioning, that wondering look fixed on their faces. Good barmen get used to it, welcome it, and affirm it. Looking for life's right thing is a very good thing.

Life's road is a great, wide boulevard on which many souls, broke, lost, insecure, and vexed as all hell, have found their way. On bar stools and behind-the-stick many of us have also discovered purpose and real joy. We have found love and found new friends, new jobs, and a new community. To everyone who enjoys a great drink, a tall tale, a smile, and a laugh across the wood, the ladies and gentlemen who inhabit and make whole this proverbial Devil's Acre, I raise my glass to you.

# NO. 12

# THE MARGARITA

*Perfected by Julio Bermejo*
*and swilled by skinny girls*
*everywhere*

## THE TOMMY'S MARGARITA

2 oz/60 ml El Tesoro tequila blanco

1 oz/30 ml fresh lime juice

1 oz/30 ml diluted agave nectar (see note)

Pour the liquid into a mixing glass, add ice, shake, then strain into a
glass—never rimmed with salt—filled with ice.

*Note: Always cut agave nectar with an equal amount of water,*
*similar to the balance of sugar and water in*
*Cocktail Syrup (page 59), before adding it to a cocktail.*

The Richmond District is a long, narrow stretch of land roughly bordered by Fulton Street to the south, the Presidio to the North, Arguello Boulevard to the east, and the Pacific Ocean to the west, with Geary Boulevard its main east-west artery. Most of the businesses in this part of the City are family owned, many of them bakeries and restaurants bearing signs in Chinese, Russian, and a few in Spanish. One of these family-owned joints is Tommy's Mexican Restaurant, which opened its doors in 1965.

To step into Tommy's is to step back in time. The decor of the many-roomed interior boasts decades-old parochial murals. The pastoral images recall another era, perhaps drawn from the experience or the imagination of the family patriarch and first owner, Tomás Bermejo. The aging, colloquial aesthetic invariably works its magic, immediately charming everyone who enters.

Many family-owned restaurants begun by first-generation Americans are like this. Their success and longevity come after a viral advocacy campaign mounted by more and more people saying, "You gotta go for the food!" This was the case for Tommy's, stuck way out in the fog, twenty blocks from the ocean.

Then things changed. Around the turn of the most recent century, Tommy's reputation evolved and people stopped going for the food alone. San Francisco began to realize that something special was happening in the little bar in Tommy's, and the food moved to a supporting role to the new star: the margaritas.

If you visited Tommy's during those days, if you actually snagged one of the highly coveted seats at the little bar, consider yourself lucky to have been a part of history. Within the always crowded bar, Tommy's son, Julio, often held forth behind-the-stick, regaling locals and visitors alike with tales of (and fueled by) tequila. We learned that Julio had long been stockpiling tequila, curating a list of vertical expressions of only 100 percent agave tequila, the same brands every year, so that now he carried the most impressive library of tequila in the United States, if not the world. He'd forbidden any expression of adulterated, or *mixto*, tequila within his domain, and his gift to the world was his bullish commitment to quality and to the telling of the story of tequila, its *terroir* and history. As he did so, always refilling the *copitas* in his guests' hands with delicious distillate, all around him young men would spin and pour and slosh margaritas back and forth from pitcher to pitcher, then finally over ice to settle.

The margaritas were stunning.

Was there a secret? At the time, yes. But now the secret ingredient to the Tommy's margarita is a standard ingredient in great cocktail bars around the world. It has become a de facto component in healthful drinking and was the inspiration for low-calorie, or "skinny," cocktails. It is also an ingredient for which I have great affinity, and passion.

In 2004, while running the cocktail program at frisson, I placed my own homespun riff on the margarita on the restaurant's cocktail menu. As I was training my team, one of the barmen stated in his inimitable way, "Why don't you just make your margarita the way Tommy's does?" I was shocked, offended, and a bit confused. I was an artist, not a mimic. I'd created this recipe organically. It was how I'd been enjoying margaritas at home for some time. Besides, what was so unique about the Tommy's margarita? I wondered. My team thought I was a hack. Maybe I am, I considered.

I am a consummate and daily drinker of tea, and years earlier I had traded out honey as a sweetener for agave nectar in my afternoon cup. I'd discovered agave nectar while living in Seattle before I was a barman, and when making cocktails at home, I'd included it. The idea of using it in a margarita made perfect sense; since mixologists experiment with different types of sugar to use in a classic daiquiri, the same should be true of using agave nectar with 100 percent agave tequila in a margarita. Then, knowing that limes in Latin America have a brighter, more floral quality than their harsh, angular counterparts most often found in the United States, I added a nip of limoncello to the other three ingredients and voila, my living room margarita.

Still, I was thought to be a hack. There was that other restaurant, an actual Mexican restaurant, run by a guy who knows a lot more about agave than I do. Julio and his Tommy's margarita were very popular, and it seemed that I was the only guy in San Francisco who didn't realize the secret was using agave nectar.

The undeniable truth is that Tommy's had been making delicious margaritas for years and had started using agave nectar in their house recipe before anyone else got hold of the stuff. They began to share this recipe with their many regulars, some of whom were evidently on my staff. Perhaps I should have paid more attention during all of the refilling of copitas and the sloshing back and forth between pitchers when I had sat at that same bar in front of Julio.

Evidently, others were listening and became believers in using agave nectar. These days, an impressive list of agave nectar brands is available in the United States, and the drink programs of multiple brands of tequila and of margarita mixes rely on the recipe conceived out in the fog on Geary Boulevard. Had it not been for this singular holistic innovation, the charisma of the Bermejo family, and the charm of the little bar where San Francisco's bartenders gathered on their nights off to eat and drink, agave nectar and its inclusion in the margarita would not have become the global phenomenon it is today.

# ON TEQUILA

Tequila has been held in high esteem for well over fifty years in San Francisco. "Tequila is a terrific drinking liquor," wrote Trader Vic Bergeron. "It tastes good; it makes a lot of wonderful flavors in mixed drinks." I include Vic's endorsement here not because it adds any particular description or further understanding of what tequila actually is, but rather because it places tequila's acceptance among local tastemakers in the past. Vic goes on to say, "One of the nicest drinks that I know how to make is a Margarita on the Rocks; it is a classic."

This ancient excitement was the result of so many Californians vacationing in Acapulco, Puerto Vallarta, and Cabo San Lucas, beautiful beach cities on Mexico's coastline just a few hours away by plane. There, you'd sit on the beach, sunning yourself, and your waiter would bring you margaritas all day long. The popularity of the margarita in Mexico was in full swing by the end of World War II, as was the blossoming career of Trader Vic. As more and more people moved to the West,

settling down in California, Nevada, and Arizona, more tequila came into the United States. The margarita followed, rising steadily to become the most popular cocktail in the country, a position it has held for decades. And it has been the success of the margarita that has driven the sales of and, ultimately, our curiosity about tequila.

So much has been written of late on the ongoing devotion to tequila and tequila producers' commitment to increasing quality that we've almost forgotten how we got started drinking shots of tequila: one-tequila, two-tequila, three-tequila, floor! Tequila, whether we knew that it was distilled from the blue agave plant (and not cactus), whether the shot came with a ridiculous little worm in the glass, or whether we remembered to lick it, suck it, then shoot it, we fell violently in love with tequila. Tequila, everyone agreed, always got the party started.

These days, the back bars of San Francisco hold only bottles of tequila that are distilled from 100 percent agave, many of which proudly proclaim their connection to the terroir of Jalisco, Mexico, to the farmers and the old families who have been in the tequila business for generations. Tequila has received more than a facelift; it went in for a full surgical brand makeover, and every bottle, that is, every brand, champions its use of original stone tools, the many years it takes for an agave plant to mature, and its slow distillation. It's a welcome, very intellectual theme, albeit a strange one: doesn't anyone remember how tequila once became the fastest-growing spirit in the United States?

Of course, the tequila I drink is among the most expensive, the most artisanal of liquid made in Mexico. I've toured the rolling valleys of Jalisco many times, visited a number of distilleries, and every time, after the careful education, the slow sipping, eventually tequila becomes tequila. You can take the worm out of the shot glass, but it's a shot of tequila that we always come back to.

## Five-Spice Margarita

*By Duggan McDonnell*

2 oz/60 ml tequila reposado

1 oz/30 ml fresh lime juice

1 oz/30 ml Chinese Five-Spice Agave
Nectar (recipe follows)

½ oz/15 ml fresh orange juice

3 dashes orange curaçao

Star anise pod for garnish

Pour the liquid into a mixing glass, add
ice, shake, then strain into a tall glass over
ice and garnish with the star anise.

## La Perla

*By Jacques Bezuidenhout, courtesy of
Dirty Habit*

1½ oz/45 ml Partida tequila reposado

1½ oz/45 ml manzanilla sherry

¾ oz/20 ml pear liqueur

Expressed lemon peel for garnish

Pour the liquid into a mixing glass, add
ice, stir forty times, then strain into a
cocktail coupe and garnish with the
lemon peel.

## Chinese Five-Spice
## Agave Nectar

2 large cinnamon sticks

1 Tbsp black peppercorns

3 star anise pods

1 cup/240 ml water

1 cup/240 ml agave nectar

One 3-in/7.5-cm piece fresh ginger,
peeled and diced

1 tsp salt

Expressed peels of 2 lemons

6 Tbsp/90 ml mezcal

In a medium saucepan, toast the
cinnamon, peppercorns, and star anise
over medium heat just until fragrant,
approximately 5 minutes. Add the water,
increase the heat to high, and bring the
mixture almost to a boil. Add the agave
nectar, ginger, salt, and lemon peels and
bring to a simmer, stirring frequently. Turn
the heat to low and simmer, continuing to
stir throughout, for 1 hour, then remove
from the heat.

Allow to cool. Spike with the mezcal,
transfer to a container, cover tightly, and
refrigerate overnight. The next day, strain
the syrup through a fine-mesh sieve into
a glass bottle or jar. The nectar is now
ready to use. Cap tightly and store in the
refrigerator for up to 3 months.

*Makes about 2 cups/480 ml*

# SUPERIOR COCKTAIL MAGUEY

We live in an era when unaged, or *blanco*, tequila can fetch upward of two hundred dollars a bottle. This is a new and frankly welcome phenomenon. If the agave plants were harvested at their peak of ripeness and the *piñas*, or hearts, of the agaves were handled correctly and then distilled properly in an alembic still, the tequila should later be served without any age from a barrel. This is the tequila most commonly enjoyed in the United States, and producers variously label it blanco, silver, or *plata*.

Blanco tequila is fresh, herbaceous, and a touch sweet, with a hint of minerality and citrus. Doesn't it sound like something you'd want in your cocktail? My motive for creating this cocktail maguey was to build on that platform of something bright and herbaceous. The very large number of agave, or maguey, varieties, includes the blue Weber agave used for tequila and the espadín agave used to produce mezcal. For this formula, start with an aromatic and unaged tequila, then layer in a rich, almost overly oaked beauty: Pueblo Viejo's Orgullo añejo. At this stage, the blend tastes and looks almost like a *reposado*. Then why not just use a reposado? Because this is a process that creates complexity. Here, we retain the freshness of the blanco as well as the rich, round vanilla and toffee notes of the añejo. Next, we layer in a little mezcal, which is produced from a different agave, and like Merlot and Cabernet, blue Weber and espadín mix together well. In addition,

the mezcal adds a note of salinity and extra herbaceousness to keep things interesting. To finish, we add a drizzle of amontillado sherry, as though the blend had been lightly finished in a sherry barrel, and then a petite splash of agave nectar to sweeten and fully bind the many molecules together.

This blend, more than many of my superior cocktail blends, benefits from plenty of blending, of aeration. I often use extra-large pitchers, or even 6-gal/23-L buckets, and I'll pour the finished blend back and forth a minimum of thirty times, before slowly and thoroughly stirring to ensure that the blend is exactly what I want it to be. *Salud!*

## The Bartender's Secret Formula: Superior Cocktail Maguey

24½ oz/700 ml tequila blanco, such as Tres Agaves

7 oz/200 ml Pueblo Viejo Orgullo añejo

3½ oz/100 ml Del Maguey VIDA mezcal

Splash of amontillado sherry

Splash of agave nectar

Blend the liquid into a large vessel, such as a 1-gal/3.8-L pitcher, noting the additional instructions given above, then allow to rest for 1 week before using.

*Makes 1 qt/1 L*

# NO. 13

## THE SAZERAC

 *Created by Antoine Peychaud and perfected in San Francisco's Peerless Saloon*

## SAZERAC

2 oz/60 ml Old Potrero rye whiskey

½ oz/15 ml Cocktail Syrup (page 59)

3 dashes absinthe

2 dashes Peychaud's bitters

2 dashes Homemade Aromatic Bitters (page 104)

Expressed lemon peel for garnish

Pour the liquid into a mixing glass, add ice, stir forty times, then strain into a rocks glass over a single stone of ice. Garnish with the lemon peel and thank God that man invented the cocktail.

To step into Elixir, at the corner of Sixteenth and Guerrero Streets, is to experience what a great neighborhood saloon can be. At only six hundred square feet, Elixir boasts more than three hundred bottlings of whiskey, plus hundreds of other spirits. The proprietor, H. Joseph Ehrmann, has had to build shelf after shelf to house his stock, to make room for his passion. There is a grain distillate for everyone inside his little room. And please don't mind the Labrador (or three) sprawled across the middle of the old wooden floor.

Long before the current renaissance of rye whiskey in the United States, the spirit was being poured aplenty throughout San Francisco. At Elixir, it has lived in the speed rail since its opening in 1858. At least that's when the saloon on this corner, this very little room, opened for the first time.

I'm sitting on a bar stool just after two o'clock in the afternoon, my forearms leaning into the mahogany. The saloon has opened early, as a Giants baseball game is being broadcast on television. I've got a Sazerac in front of me, and it's not long for this world.

The Sazerac is a cocktail of distinctly New Orleans origin: bright, bold—and, yes—with bitters. It is also beloved in San Francisco. A proper Sazerac is composed of several fingers of rye, one finger of cocktail syrup, and petite dashes of absinthe and Peychaud's bitters, all heartily stirred so as to be bitingly cold, then strained off into a glass and garnished with a freshly expressed lemon peel dropped into the brew. When made just right, the Sazerac isn't all that complicated, doesn't take that much time, yet it stands as a sophisticated booze bomb guaranteed to slay any drinker.

I order a second Sazerac and watch the young lady behind the wood quickly spin the bottles, lifting, pouring, then stirring and straining. It takes the lass thirty seconds to produce—thirty seconds, as though it were as common to her as a rum and Coke—and there again in front of me was the strong but gentle masterpiece.

The original Sazerac conceived in New Orleans was an ethnic cocktail, using ingredients of entirely French extraction: Cognac, absinthe, and Peychaud's Bitters. Back then, whiskey wasn't employed in the Sazerac; rather it was Cognac, the esteemed brandy from France. New Orleans was and still is connected to its French roots, and Cognac came into its port with abandon.

A plausible theory exists that rye whiskey came to be substituted for Cognac in the Sazerac in New Orleans when phylloxera raged in Europe, devastating her vineyards and thus the production of Cognac, and it makes a fair bit of sense. The amount of Cognac arriving in the Port of New Orleans had significantly diminished, yet the taste for the Sazerac continued to grow. Somewhere, in some bar, someone must have poured rye whiskey that had come down the Mississippi River for the increasingly unavailable Cognac. It sounds like a respectable anthropology-based story.

Except the narrative has a few holes in it. The first (and still remaining) recipe ever published for the Sazerac came from San Francisco's own "Cocktail Bill" Boothby. Now as then, there is much cross-pollination between the robust eating and drinking communities of San Francisco and New Orleans. Our citizens vacation in each other's city, our bars share ideas, employees, and cultural references. There is reason to assume that Boothby might have received the secret recipe for a rye whiskey Sazerac from a New Orleans barkeep. Or, there is the fact that Johnny Farley's Peerless Saloon on Market Street was famous for serving its Gold Rush Sazerac made especially with rye whiskey instead of Cognac. This was the San Francisco of the Gay Nineties, a wild city at its wildest, which had exchanged commerce and customs with New Orleans for fifty years. But the name of the drink is telling; the actual gold rush had long passed. Had this drink been popular for decades in San Francisco, and had it long been served with the far less expensive spirit most consumed by gold miners? It seems likely, as whiskey, along with brandy, were the two most popular locally distilled spirits in old California.

When Boothby put the first recipe for a Sazerac to paper, he wasn't just referencing a classic peculiar to another community. No, the Sazerac had been well known and enjoyed in San Francisco, and the City had made the cocktail her own long before he recorded it.

# NO. 14

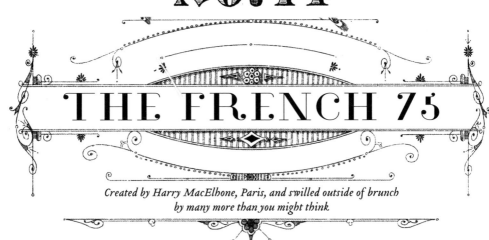

## THE FRENCH 75

*Created by Harry MacElhone, Paris, and swilled outside of brunch
by many more than you might think*

## FRENCH 75

*Adapted by Ian Adams from a recipe by Harry MacElhone*

1 oz/30 ml G'Vine gin

1 oz/30 ml Armagnac

1 oz/30 ml fresh lemon juice

½ oz/15 ml Cocktail Syrup (page 59)

1 oz/30 ml sparkling wine

Expressed lemon peel for garnish

Pour the gin, Armagnac, lemon juice, and cocktail syrup into a mixing
glass, add ice, shake briefly, then strain into a tall glass over ice while
simultaneously pouring in the wine as a lift. Garnish with the lemon peel
and be glad that you found this drink. It's a dream.

After reading the recipe for the French 75, you might think it is just a brunch cocktail, something slightly sweet, lighter, hardly bracing at all. That's not necessarily true. Yes, the French 75 is a quick sip and altogether refreshing, but if you're not careful, its elegance will bite back.

Harry's New York Bar, Paris, is the birthplace of the French 75, and to alight atop a bar stool inside its environs and sip a French 75 is a pilgrimage for any barkeep worth his salt. Plus, it's a damn fine way to spend an afternoon enjoying great drink.

As I've mentioned, San Francisco holds much in common with Paris and has also been touted by many as America's most European city. My cousins and friends of mine who live in Paris love San Francisco, and, hey, what's not to like about Paris? The city and the French have given the world a particular style—a high style that permeates not just fashion but also Champagne and chocolate and cocktails. If I were to open another cocktail saloon, I'd think hard about Latin America, say Lima or Buenos Aires, yet the siren of Paris is hard to silence. Paris is so beautiful and always so smart that to sling drinks there would be sublime.

Harry's New York Bar in Paris is the equivalent of San Francisco's Bank Exchange Saloon in that it has had multiple owners over a period of generations, but it was one man, a bartender, who made all the difference. Like Duncan Nicol, Harry MacElhone came up through the ranks, moving from barman (he was the opening barman in 1911) to proprietor (he took the bar over in 1923), and was equally, if not more, talented than Duncan. He was an ingenious marketer and told the stories of his drinks and his cocktail saloon very, very well. Harry's Bar was never the Ritz, but Papa Hemingway and many lads of the Jazz Age, including boxing champ Jack Dempsey, who later was the bouncer in what is now the City's Comstock Saloon, all made the pilgrimage to see Harry. Cocktail lovers have continued to make their way to the famed spot, first to see Harry's son and then his grandson and today his great-grandson, who currently tends to the bar.

Over the years, the barmen of Harry's New York Bar created many classic cocktails that are now much loved in San Francisco, among them the sidecar (page 117), the Bloody Mary (page 111), and, of course, the French 75, to name but three.

When you walk into Harry's Bar, you might mistake it for a university club or, perhaps, for any saloon hosting a reunion of the Yale Alumni Association. Collegiate pennants and shields are hung the length of the long, mahogany-paneled room, and glass display cases hold various plaques and other sporting memorabilia. In other words, Harry's has a lot of history and it's all on display.

But make no mistake, the aesthetic works, and once you have perched yourself atop an old wooden bar stool and are cherishing the first famous drink created in this room, the French 75, you'll agree. The barman builds the drink in a tall glass, the kind employed at Absinthe back in San Francisco for the *citron pressé*. He layers in gin, followed by lemon juice, cocktail syrup, a dash or two of absinthe, and then he lifts the mix with bubbly before adding ice, giving the cocktail a petite stir, and finally sliding it across the wood into your hands.

This was my experience, and as the tall glass came toward me, just a little shiver, *un petit frisson*, ran through my body. Gripping the glass tenderly, I sipped from the tall straw and . . . wow. You see, I cannot begin to count how many French 75s I've slung when I have tended bar five, six nights a week. For an era, perhaps a decade or more, the French 75 was a cocktail of absolute delicious importance, reigning on cocktail menus throughout San Francisco (and not just at brunch). The City's top mixologists agreed that the French 75 was the quintessential drink to get vodka consumers on to the drinking of gin. In 2004, you'd see the French 75 on San Francisco cocktail menus, and to be sure, many folks were ordering them at eleven o'clock on a Saturday night. Was it the festive flute in which the drink was often served? It could be. Was it that the drink tasted so similar to San Francisco's lemon drop but with a float of Champagne? *Ab-so-fucking-lutely*. So mixologists saw the French 75 as the perfect gateway drug: Get a customer on to drinking the French 75 and next comes the aviation cocktail, perhaps then a Pisco sour, and down the road just a bit, a last word will delight. From that point on, the guest will trust you, the barkeep, completely.

So there I was amid the pennants and lore of Harry's Bar, sucking back my French 75. It was fine, and a perfectly balanced cocktail that somehow went down too quickly. Was that the point, a point that I had just realized?

In Paris at Harry's, the drink is served tall over ice and it contains only gin, not brandy. You see, there has been a debate of history about whether the drink was actually first made with, of course, French Cognac, not gin. Now, the wonder of this cocktail is that it works wondrously with both gin and Cognac, and there are certainly a few folks who prefer the version with brandy. Then again, we also have the ultracreative outlier, Ian Adams, head barman at 15 Romolo, which sits just above the Hungry I strip club off Broadway back in San Francisco, who prepares the French 75 by splitting the booze between gin and Armagnac. Ian is a City native and can't be fooled. "There is a debate over which spirit originated or, perhaps, is better in the cocktail. I thought, let's put them together and just celebrate the drink."

Amen.

# MAKE YOUR OWN
# MEYER LEMON MARMALADE

The Meyer lemon is a unique and practically ideal fruit. It is a smaller, sweeter lemon than the more common Eureka and Lisbon varieties, and it typically matures without a blemish on its skin. The Meyer's color rises from pale green to popcorn blonde to a bold gold, at which point it is ready for picking.

Throughout Northern California, the Meyer lemon is regarded as the perfect citrus. One of these faithful is Karen Morss, who planted a veritable orchard of the citrus in her southward-facing backyard in Redwood City, a forty-five-minute drive south of the City. Karen is a retired pilot and former corporate executive who fell in love with the Meyer lemon, which she is quick to describe. "I love Meyer lemons. I still remember the very first time I tasted one. Pure bliss! They are so sweet that you can eat them without puckering."

From the day I opened Cantina, I was sourcing local citrus. A fair portion of what I would gather came from the backyards of family and friends throughout the Bay Area. I would bring a barkeep or two with me and we would climb among the branches picking Meyers, tangerines, oranges, and grapefruits galore. Then, in the winter of 2007, Karen emailed me to say that she had read in the *San Francisco Chronicle* that mine was a bar that carried and gave a damn about local citrus, and she asked if I might be interested in purchasing some of hers.

I didn't need much convincing. Her orchard is beautiful and her fruit superb. In the beginning, Karen passed her Meyer lemon marmalade along to me. It was unique, different, and at first, I was critical, dismissive. You see, I'd grown up on orange marmalade, and that taste acquired in childhood I now fervently employed in cocktail recipes. Karen's Meyer lemon marmalade is sweeter and so it bears a slightly higher sugar density. Foolish me, I thought it would perform just like plain ol' orange marmalade, but in fact it was much better.

# MEYER LEMON MARMALADE
### By Karen Morss

4 cups/950 g sliced Meyer lemons
4 cups/960 ml water
4 cups/800 g sugar, plus more if needed
½ cup/120 ml fresh Meyer lemon juice

Prep by halving the lemons crosswise and removing all the seeds. Gather the seeds onto a square of cheesecloth, bring the corners of the square together, and tie securely with kitchen string. Cut each lemon half into quarters and thinly slice the quarters ¼ in/6 mm thick. Combine the lemons with the bag of seeds in a large nonreactive pot, add the water, cover, and let stand at room temperature for 24 hours.

Put two or three saucers in the freezer. Uncover the pot, place it over medium heat, and slowly bring the lemon mixture to a boil. When it begins to boil, turn the heat to medium-low and cook, uncovered, for 45 minutes. Begin to skim off foam as it accumulates. Stir in the sugar and lemon juice, adjust the heat to medium, and cook, stirring occasionally. Continue to skim the foam. When the sugar has fully dissolved, taste and add a little more sugar if necessary (add only ¼ cup/50 g at a time). Cook until a small spoonful of marmalade pulled from the pot and dropped onto a chilled saucer and left for about 30 seconds gels, at least 30 minutes longer. If it fails to gel, cook for 5 to 10 minutes longer and test again.

Meanwhile, preheat the oven to 250°F/120°C and put at least six ½-pt/ 240-ml canning jars in the oven for 15 minutes. When the marmalade is ready, remove the jars from the oven and leave the oven on. Ladle the hot marmalade into the jars, filling each jar to within ¼ in/6 mm of the rim. Wipe the rims clean with a dampened cloth and top each jar with a lid and ring band. Return the filled jars to the heated oven for 15 minutes, then transfer them to a wire rack to cool. Check each cooled jar for a good seal by pressing the center of the lid with a fingertip. If the lid springs upward when you remove your finger, the seal is not good. Refrigerate the jar and use the marmalade within 3 months.

Store the jars at room temperature for up to 6 months. Refrigerate each jar after opening.

*Makes about six ½-pt/240-ml jars*

## Meyer Lemon 75

*By Duggan McDonnell*

2 oz/60 ml California brandy

Rounded 1 Tbsp Meyer lemon marmalade, homemade (see page 159) or store-bought

½ oz/15 ml fresh lemon juice

½ oz/15 ml Cocktail Syrup (page 59)

1 oz/30 ml sparkling wine

Put the brandy, marmalade, lemon juice, and cocktail syrup into a mixing glass, add ice, shake vigorously, then fine-strain into a Champagne flute while simultaneously pouring in the wine as a lift. This beauty doesn't need a garnish.

## Cherry Bounce

*Adapted by Jonny Raglin, courtesy of Comstock Saloon*

2 oz/60 ml bourbon

1 oz/30 ml fresh lemon juice

1 oz/30 ml juice from brandied cherries

½ oz/15 ml Cocktail Syrup (page 59)

2 dashes aromatic bitters, homemade (see page 104) or store-bought

1 oz/30 ml sparkling wine

Pour the bourbon, lemon juice, cherry juice, cocktail syrup, and bitters into a mixing glass, add ice, shake briefly, then strain into a cocktail glass while simultaneously pouring in the wine as a lift.

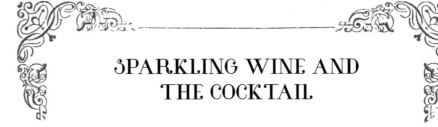

# SPARKLING WINE AND THE COCKTAIL

Pray tell, what does a little doubly fermented wine offer a cocktail? The answer is either perfection or simply dilution. The addition of any sparkling wine to a cocktail needs to be a well-reasoned decision. That means that you must determine that the bubbly will make the cocktail much better. If not, well, skip it.

The successful use of sparkling wine in cocktails gets into chemistry and the subjects of Brix and pH balance, which is why fermented bubbles can make a drink fantastic or ruin it. And I've insisted that my students learn when it is okay to pour.

In the case of the French 75, the cocktail that exists before the bubbles are introduced tastes similar to a gin gimlet, a gin-ish lemon drop, or a thin aviation. It's a fair cocktail but one that won't deliver you to heaven. The French 75 needed a literal and figurative lift; hence, the Champagne. The bubbles add sugar and effervescence and a little dryness, creating a youthful wonder in the glass and on your palate.

To add a little bubbly to a cocktail is a celebratory delight, but it ain't a sure thing. Remember what "Cocktail Bill" Boothby did to his beloved Manhattan; he tweaked the recipe, and only then did he lift it with tiny bubbles. For the French 75, and every other sparkling cocktail, follow Boothby's example.

# NO. 15

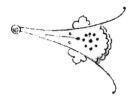

# THE SMASH

*Perfected by Harry Johnson and Duggan McDonnell as an
homage to the world's first drink*

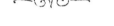

## SMASH

*Adapted from a recipe
by Harry Johnson*

3 lemon slices

3 lime slices

10 fresh mint leaves

3 small fresh basil leaves

2 oz/60 ml spirit of choice

1 oz/30 ml Cocktail Syrup (page 59)

Muddle the produce together in a mixing glass, then pour in the
spirit and cocktail syrup, add ice, and shake vigorously.
Pour all into a tall glass and celebrate.

That old cocktail—that original farm-to-glass mosaic—the smash is my inspiration for every moment spent leaning steady against the wood, shaking, stirring, smashing! My God, I love her. California brandy? No, it'll be rum. No, make it whiskey. No, Pisco, with muddled citrus galore, a nip of ginger, and a hint of savory basil, all brightened with cocktail syrup. Shaken hard, almost to injury, then the smash is ready and poured entirely into a tall glass flush and wet and whole—like a Caipirinha, a julep, a sangria. Pop the surface with a straw and suck. What you're tasting is a fantastic delight inspired by either South America or California that brings together fresh fruit and spirit violently and thoroughly in the world's first cocktail.

Harry Johnson recorded the first recipe for a smash, and some think the concept was taken from the julep. It's true that the American South had to have produced some effect on Johnson, as he claimed to have won the country's first ever barman's cocktail competition, which was held in New Orleans. But remember that Johnson first tended bar in San Francisco, which blossomed out of contact with Latin America to become perhaps the most ethnically diverse city in the United States in those days. Fresh fruit and boozy punches—essentially smashes—were how Californians had enjoyed spirits long before Harry ever stepped behind a bar.

The smash, so very old, makes us think twice about cocktail history. All too often our American history focuses on our own internal sources of information rather than on those of other cultures. The truth just might be found elsewhere: the world's first "cocktail" or "punch" or "hooch" was not created here in the United States, unless you count the mixological efforts of Sir Francis Drake on the beach in Northern California. Aha, but then, the Draquecito was in fact a smash!

Our country's modern language for cocktails is young, having originated hundreds of years after booze and fruit came together in a cup in Latin America. Our hemisphere's first distilled spirit occurred in either Coahuila, Mexico, or Lima, Peru, as both regions began harvesting vines and producing a single distilled grape spirit to fortify their wines by the 1530s, However, it was Peru's little port town of Pisco and its surrounding region that desired and created a culture of distillation first. It is true that geographic regions of distillation are bountiful, producing many fruits and vegetables to accompany the distilling of wine. And it is logical to assume that these sources of distillation in the New World birthed the first mixed drink in which spirit and fresh fruit came together. Ask yourself how you consumed your first distilled spirit? Was it in a mixed drink or was it neat, the spirit on its own? If you are among the majority of Americans who first drank rum within a rum and Coke, did you in fact know what rum was and did it matter? Did your consumption of rum flourish afterward, always mixed with Coke?

Did not the Peruvians and Mexicans of the sixteenth century enjoy their aguardiente de vino with fresh mango, lime, pineapple, and mint as they do today? Did they care and know that they were drinking an American cocktail? Of course not, since the history of both Mexico and Peru predates that of both the United States and our word *cocktail*.

Alas, I digress. What's important to grasp here is that the smash is an umbrella term for a type of mixed drink (or cocktail) that is our earliest form of boozy tipple.

* * *

When I step into the well at the top of a shift, I think about this history, about Harry Johnson, a muddler in his right hand, smashing up the bounty of California at the bottom of a copper mug. I think about the great history of drinks that even Harry did not know about. More important, I think of how I can make the best, simplest drink for the guest right in front of me, which often involves fresh fruit, even if only a citrus expressed for its peel.

This particular smash, as I see it, is the holy and ecumenical connection of fruit and spirit, a wild and wholly mortal combination that made God smile. A smash can, in fact, have lemon verbena, raspberries, apricots, peppercorns, and so much more because, well, it's a smash. And if cocktails are a smashing success these days, it is to the smash that we should show our gratitude.

# A BARKEEP'S WHIMSY

A cocktail menu is but a road map, a trick, a piece of bait to bring people into a lair. Once in, the game is to keep, to hold on to every guest in the room. Folks visit saloons because of the cocktail menu, because the printed piece of paper proclaims *fresh, smart, classic*. I've written more than a few menus, and it's a serious pursuit, that is, as long as you think it is.

The menu is a piece of marketing and a little billboard of education telling the guest what the house is good at. It is by no means all that the barkeeps are capable of slinging. In fact, a great menu should communicate the overall array of the bar's offerings and the broad talents of the bar's team.

On menus these days, you'll see a bit of language that might read "Dealer's Choice" or "Barkeep's Whimsy." This style of *omakase* service is increasingly popular and allows the barkeep a little freedom to create something new following the suggestions of the guest.

## Blackberry and Cabernet Caipirinha
*By Duggan McDonnell*

6 lime slices

2 orange slices

3 blackberries

2 oz/60 ml cachaça, such as Leblon

1 oz/30 ml California Cabernet

1 oz/30 ml Cocktail Syrup (page 59)

Muddle the produce in a mixing glass, then pour in the liquid, add ice, and shake vigorously. Pour all into a large glass and serve.

# THE PISCO SOUR

*Created by Victor Morris, Lima, Peru, or perhaps by an
unknown barkeep on the Barbary Coast*

## PISCO SOUR

1 egg white

2 oz/60 ml Campo de Encanto Grand & Noble Pisco

1 oz/30 ml fresh lime juice

1 oz/30 ml Cocktail Syrup (page 59)

Dash aromatic bitters, homemade (see page 104)
or store-bought

Pour the egg white, Pisco, lime juice, and cocktail syrup into a mixing
glass, add only a few cubes of ice, then shake vigorously until the
ice is nearly depleted. Fine-strain into a goblet, garnish with
the single dash of bitters, and exhale.

Barkeeps throughout Northern California will attest that they have shaken many a Pisco sour. It is the egg white cocktail of choice and an absolutely beloved one by most. Long before I got into the Pisco business, I cherished the Pisco sour. I especially liked drinking one when beginning a night of cocktails, and I regularly suggested them to guests, especially novices, squeamish about drinking a cocktail with a raw egg white in it.

As much as San Francisco loves its Pisco sours, Lima loves the drink even more. When you land at Jorge Chávez International Airport in the capital, you can immediately head to the bar—after clearing customs, that is. Peru's national drink is a delicious, ubiquitous concoction that is served in every bar in the country, even those in provincial bus stations, as I have experienced.

A few years ago, in an effort to promote Campo de Encanto, I participated in the three-day Pisco Sour Festival in Lima. It was a very civilized affair in an urban park, even though we were going through hundreds of eggs and limes each day. Despite those numbers, business wasn't brisk. There was never a line. The Peruvians are a proud, polite people, but this was a cocktail festival, and I wanted to create a little ruckus for the brand. I loaded hip-hop and R&B songs on my laptop, bought a small set of speakers, and set up shop as deejay in our little tent. Then, I instructed the American and Australian barkeeps who had traveled with me to shake those sours shirtless.

It worked. Latin America's most elegant cocktail, frothy, balanced, bright yet rich, came served tall after being heartily shaken with biceps and pectorals on view. Soon a line formed, the cameras came out, and the music got louder. Next, Peruvians were stepping behind Encanto's bar to have their photo taken with the young, shirtless men. Hundreds of photos were snapped, the television cameras arrived, and so too did the police. The shirts, they said, needed to be put back on.

The festival for the most ubiquitous drink in the country had received a little burst of energy. It needed that boost because the Pisco sour is so common in Peru that it can, at times, cease to be a sublime creation. Many Peruvians attribute the decline in its quality to the use of a blender or to the fact that it is a very forgiving cocktail. With sugar, egg white, and fresh citrus, even a paltry Pisco can still make a fair sour. And that is probably what has happened—thousands of times each day throughout Peru, inferior products come together, are rapidly blended, and then heaped into a glass.

But I also wonder whether Peru's cocktail culture has become overly reliant on the sour. Peru is still waiting to birth a hearty cocktail culture, replete with many additional classics. That lack of variety, the discipline and palate required to make many different cocktails on an ongoing basis, hasn't kept the Pisco sour distinct or precise. I shared this perspective with Rick Vecchio, an American journalist living in Peru, who then shared a bit of his research, which enlightened, if not altered, my perspective on the Pisco sour.

Rick handed me a clipping from an old English-language newspaper printed in Peru, the *West Coast Leader*. The article, which was dated January 8, 1921, read: "Pisco, the beverage (and beverage is a very mild term by which to identify it as a drink), is internationally famous; but Pisco, the port, is little known, outside shipping circles. One well-known saloon on the 'Barbary Coast,' in the old pre-Volstead days in San Francisco, was famous for its 'Pisco Sours'; but probably not one person in ten thousand who drank Pisco in San Francisco had ever heard of the Peruvian port of that name."

The newspaper was printed at the height of the popularity of the Morris Bar in Lima, Peru, where American Victor Morris supposedly invented the sour sometime after opening the bar in 1916. The *West Coast Leader* attributes the popularity (but not the origin) of the Pisco sour to San Francisco before the 1906 earthquake and fire that permanently eradicated the slums and saloons of the Barbary Coast. The famed Bank Exchange Saloon sat at the border of the Barbary Coast and was very often lumped with the region. Could the Bank Exchange have been the saloon the author references in the article?

The origin of the Pisco sour may well have been in San Francisco in the late nineteenth century, a time during which the whiskey sour was plentiful and ubiquitous across the country. Then along came the great egg white delight, the silver fizz by Harry Johnson. Put that innovation together with the fact that Pisco was heralded as a special spirit in the City of San Francisco, and quickly it seems that the Pisco sour originated in the same domain as so many other classic cocktails. The primary evidence is that long-ago quote from Peru's *West Coast Leader* pointing to the drink's popularity in old San Francisco. Anything further would be hearsay or folklore, such as a tale from the mouth of a barkeep. Hardly reliable!

Then, too, Vic Morris never claimed to have invented the Pisco sour, plus plenty of cocktails containing egg whites were being consumed in San Francisco before the arrival of the twentieth century, before the Pisco sour first appeared at the Morris Bar in Lima. Replacing gin or whiskey with Pisco where fizzes and sours were shaken with such active abandon seems like a natural evolution, especially in the spiritual home of Pisco, San Francisco. Remember that the mai tai wasn't invented in Tahiti or even Hawaii, so if the Pisco sour came from San Francisco, stranger things have happened. Furthermore, plenty of Westerners traveled back and forth along the Pacific between San Francisco and Lima. Included in that set were a few bartenders, specifically the employees of the Bank Exchange Saloon, who signed the registry of the Morris Bar. Might these vacationing San Francisco barkeeps have shared a recipe or two with the proprietor of the Morris Bar?

Does Latin America's most elegant cocktail actually have her roots in San Francisco?

Allow me to remind you: San Francisco had not long been out of Latin America when this burst of cocktail creativity occurred, and the oldest-surviving written record of the word *Pisco* in California dates to 1830, before the territory was in the United States.

My research yielded yet another wrinkle in the narrative of this cocktail's origin. The San Francisco author of the *Pisco Trail*, Nico Vera, unearthed a cookbook titled *Nuevo Manual de Cocina a la Criolla*, published in Lima in 1903. In this Spanish-language volume, Nico found a recipe for a drink titled simply "Cocktail," which called for the following ingredients: "An egg white, a glass of Pisco, a teaspoon of fine sugar, and a few drops of lime as desired." Those are the exact ingredients for a Pisco sour, which makes Vera's discovery the oldest written record for a cocktail with these ingredients.

So now we have multiple references to the origin of the Pisco sour. The earliest record seems to point to San Francisco, but then it is entirely possible that the "Cocktail" that came to be the Pisco sour—whether it was influenced by San Francisco or not—had been prepared for a reasonable time in Lima before being included in a cookbook. Where was the first Pisco sour made? We'll never know.

If the Pisco sour has her roots in San Francisco, she still belongs to Peru. My favorite drink to sip while in New Orleans is the imported Pimm's cup, near and dear to the heart of the French Quarter. And let's not forget San Francisco's devotion to the imported Negroni. This Pisco sour, whether born in or adopted by San Francisco, remains Latin America's most elegant cocktail.

## Silver Fizz
*By Harry Johnson*

1 egg white

2 oz/60 ml Old Tom gin

1 oz/30 ml fresh lemon juice

1 oz/30 ml Cocktail Syrup (page 59)

1 oz/30 ml seltzer

Pour the egg white, gin, lemon juice, and cocktail syrup into a mixing glass, add ice, shake vigorously, then strain into a highball glass. Lift with the seltzer before serving.

## Blue Ribbon Sour
*By Duggan McDonnell*

2 egg whites

2 oz/60 ml Campo de Encanto Grand & Noble Pisco

1 oz/30 ml fresh lime juice

½ oz/15 ml rich sherry

¾ oz/20 ml Cocktail Syrup (page 59)

Expressed orange peel for garnish

Pour the egg whites and liquid into a mixing glass, add ice, shake vigorously, then fine-strain into a goblet. Express the orange peel over the cocktail, then toss the peel aside and enjoy the luxury.

## Rattlesnake
*By Harry Craddock and adapted by Thad Vogler, courtesy of Bar Agricole*

1 egg white

2 oz/60 ml rye whiskey

1 oz/30 ml fresh lemon juice

½ oz/15 ml maple syrup

2 dashes Peychaud's bitters

Expressed lemon peel for garnish

Pour the egg white and liquid into a mixing glass, add ice, shake vigorously, then fine-strain into a cocktail coupe. Garnish with the lemon peel.

# WAITER, THERE'S AN EGG IN MY COCKTAIL!

If only the egg, like gum arabic in a syrup, were a secret unseen trick. The egg is still a controversial subject in cocktails, as public health departments across the country warn against using fresh eggs in cocktails for fear of salmonella.

Crack open an egg and allow the white to ooze away from the yolk, letting gravity do the work for you. That egg white is thick, viscous, and different from the yolk in that it does not deliver much flavor, making it perfect for cocktails.

Make yourself a sour without the egg white and you'll be sorely disappointed. Many of the flavor molecules are present, but the reward is missing. The protein of the egg white delivers all the viscosity for which the Pisco sour is so rightly loved. The white of the egg expands when shaken, falls apart, and then reattaches itself to the other molecules within the cocktail to create a newly bonded, wholly rapturous mouthfeel. Make yourself a margarita with an egg white in it; now, do it again, this time with two egg whites in it. Egg whites in cocktails are what bacon and salt are to food: they make everything taste better.

In the grocery stores of Lima, Peru, eggs are displayed on the shelves nearest to the cash registers, the same spot where Snickers, 3 Musketeers, and other candy bars are kept in the States. I don't fully understand this, nor do I grasp why the eggs are kept unrefrigerated and all is fine, while in the States we are advised never to leave eggs at room temperature. Nonetheless, these room-temperature displays do explain the custom of adding aromatic bitters to a Pisco sour. Warm eggs have a different aroma than refrigerated eggs. The smell does not indicate that they are bad; it just means that their natural aroma has not been subdued by refrigeration. Thus, floating a dash of spice on a Pisco sour will combat the odor of sulfur that can creep up in any cocktail with egg white in it. In San Francisco, we rarely encounter this sulfurous edge, so serving a Pisco sour without bitters is perfectly acceptable. Further, it is mere decoration to create elaborate designs with bitters atop a sour; they may look pretty, but the delicate balance of flavor of the cocktail will be thrown off by that addition of bitters.

Last but not least, adding an egg white to a cocktail helps to enhance a rich balance on the palate. It delivers a visceral, rather than a flavor-forward, experience. That means that getting the acid-to-sugar balance correct is essential. Remember, the Pisco sour is a forgiving cocktail. When acid and sugar are balanced, the alcohol integrates into the story. It is evidence that a tart Pisco sour is never a good Pisco sour. Sugar and alcohol used separately are ingredients that will punch flavor; together they can work miracles (hence, the creation of the cocktail). Setting the correct ratio of alcohol, acid, and sugar in every sour before adding the egg white will ensure that the final iteration of the cocktail will deliver liquid velvet on the palate.

500 Block Pacific Avenue (north side on left looking east) House of Pisco, 1946

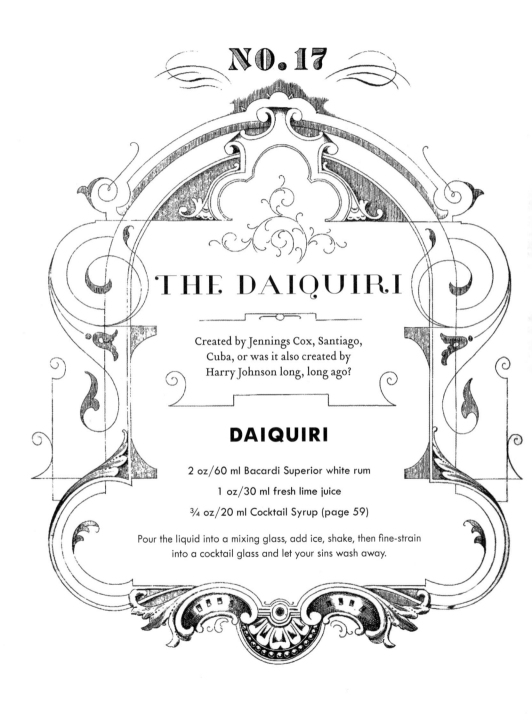

# THE DAIQUIRI

Created by Jennings Cox, Santiago,
Cuba, or was it also created by
Harry Johnson long, long ago?

## DAIQUIRI

2 oz/60 ml Bacardi Superior white rum

1 oz/30 ml fresh lime juice

¾ oz/20 ml Cocktail Syrup (page 59)

Pour the liquid into a mixing glass, add ice, shake, then fine-strain
into a cocktail glass and let your sins wash away.

The classic daiquiri, that is, the simplest version of the drink, is a vexing delight. These days, the recipe for and understanding of a classic dry daiquiri are that it has just three ingredients: white rum, fresh lime juice, and sugar. With something so simple, how could anything go wrong? Therein lies the mixologist's conundrum. The daiquiri demands a perfect ratio of ingredients to play in harmony. With so many great mixologists in San Francisco, taking up the cause of the perfect daiquiri became a call to arms during this cocktail renaissance. It also became an effort to redefine the daiquiri as something not born of a blender with strawberries and ice cream and more. When shaken right, the daiquiri, like the gimlet and San Francisco's Tommy's margarita, is a concoction of lean perfection.

San Francisco is partly to blame for the daiquiri's identity crisis. The cocktail itself, its original recipe, the very name and all its lore, is of extremely nebulous origin, as no one can agree who first came up with the tipple. Needless to say, it has since morphed into a family of drinks, a platform of rum, citrus, and sweetener that lent itself to the imagination. Enter, Henry Africa.

In the 1970s, Norman Hobday aimed to deliver a spectacularly unique bar in San Francisco. The era of Trader Vic Bergeron was at its height of popularity, but Vic was only catering to the hoity-toity high society of Nob Hill and Pacific Heights. He'd gone over and was no longer a barman of the people. Hobday wanted to create a bar for the people, something fun, imaginative, relevant. Alas, he had very little money.

The success of Henry Africa's bar was tied to three things: Hobday and his cult of personality, his choice of decor, and his menu of many-flavored daiquiris. (Oh, the fact that the young Harry Denton later played piano in the loft above the doorway might have helped, too.) Hobday borrowed just enough dough to open the place, and decided to hang ferns from the ceiling in place of more expensive furnishings. That idea transformed Henry Africa's into the very first fern bar, later copied by many other bars in San Francisco. Once the doors were open, Hobday lobbed loads of ice cream into his blender and marketed his daiquiri menu to the ladies. His plan worked.

In no time at all, Henry Africa's became the hottest bar in town, packed to the rafters with women slurping ice-cream daiquiris amid the lush jungle of potted plants. The guys soon followed, started buying the daiquiris for all the gals, and Hobday, who'd changed his name to Henry Africa, got rich. The net effect for the daiquiri, however, was that it became nothing like the cocktail it once was. And so the true daiquiri, bright and dry, crisp and simple, was forgotten.

Nearly a generation of barkeeps ignored the daiquiri because of the confusion it wrought on their bars when the mere mention of the cocktail to a guest invited questions about the many flavor possibilities. The stern and classically composed barkeep would frown, perhaps offer a scorn-filled lecture on the real daiquiri, and then leave his or her guest in an equally unpleasant mood.

One of the stories about the original daiquiri conceived by interloping journalist Jennings Cox in far-off Cuba is that it contained both light and dark rums, lime or lemon juice, sugar, and shaved ice. That is the exact list of ingredients in Harry Johnson's St. Croix rum punch of 1882. And a daiquiri with a nip of aged rum is fantastic.

The cocktail renaissance of the first decade of this century has rightfully restored the classic daiquiri. We no longer quibble over its origin, just its balance on the palate. How can three ingredients cause so much trouble? The simple answer is that none of the trio—rum, sugar, lime—is a simple, consistent ingredient. A rum distilled in Venezuela will always taste different from a rum distilled in Puerto Rico. Limes harvested in Brazil are vastly different from those grown in Oaxaca, Mexico, and when either lime arrives in the States, how it matures and dries, becoming less sweet and more acidic, will always affect the cocktail in which it is used. And then there is the choice of sugar. You may differ from me and choose to use a dry, light sugar in your daiquiri, or you may prefer a richer brown sugar–based syrup for this cocktail. So, you see, the daiquiri, which is always popular in its many incarnations from San Francisco to Cuba and back, remains an ever-vexing, ever-delicious delight.

## St. Croix Rum Punch

*By Harry Johnson*

1½ oz/45 ml Cruzan light (white) rum

½ oz/15 ml Mount Gay XO rum

¾ oz/20 ml fresh lemon juice

¾ oz/20 ml Cocktail Syrup (page 59)

Pour the liquid into a mixing glass, add ice, shake, then strain into a goblet over crushed ice.

## Hemingway

*By Papa and adapted by Duggan McDonnell*

2 oz/60 ml Matusalem Platino rum

1 oz/30 ml fresh Ruby Red grapefruit juice

¾ oz/20 ml Cocktail Syrup (page 59)

½ oz/15 ml fresh lime juice

¼ oz/10 ml maraschino liqueur

Pour the liquid into a mixing glass, add ice, shake, then fine-strain into a cocktail glass.

# SUPERIOR COCKTAIL RUM

"What one rum can't do, three rums can," quipped Donn Beach. Beach, by way of New Orleans, became Los Angeles's greatest cocktail talent by fortifying his imagination and altering his identity from Ernest Gant and becoming colloquially known as Don the Beachcomber. But he not only made a great punch, he was also a master blender. His comment on the power of three rums resonates with me, in particular for this blend of cocktail rum.

Rum, the distilled essence of sugarcane or its by-product, molasses, can be produced anywhere in the world. To then create a dynamic, complex blend is highly possible and easily achieved. The layers of distilled molasses on fresh sugarcane on the vanilla and tobacco gleaned from time in barrels are playfully delicious. Rum has an association with whimsy, and it is also the spirit that binds the many territories of the New World together. In this cocktail rum, Puerto Rico is blended with Martinique and Venezuela and Jamaica. Each rum is unique, yet together they deliver a harmony from a much stronger chorus.

That's definitely what Donn Beach was getting at. There is also much historical precedent for it. Rum has always been a blended spirit, even inside the old taverns of New England where the tails—the the last droppings—of every barrel, were blended together to sell for a few extra

bucks. The resulting glug, which was sold from its own barrel through the cock, or spigot, was known as the "cock's tail."

Cheers!

## The Bartender's Secret Formula: Superior Cocktail Rum

24½ oz/700 ml Matusalem Platino rum

3½ oz/100 ml French rhum agricole, such as Clément or La Favorite

3½ oz/100 ml Venezuelan aged rum, such as Santa Teresa or Diplomático

3½ oz/100 ml Appleton Estate V/X rum

Blend the liquid into a large vessel, such as a 1-gal/3.8-L pitcher, then allow to rest for 1 week before using.

*Makes 1 qt/1 L*

*Interior of Carlo's Restaurant and Bar, December 31, 1941*

# Latin Cocktails Are Best in the Winter

The season for fresh citrus frustrates saloon keepers every year. Each summer, with the weather heating up, patrons begin requesting more and more margaritas, mojitos, Caipirinhas, Pisco punches, and on and on. But Mother Nature doesn't cooperate exactly as we'd like her to. You see, citrus crops are harvested in the winter, and when June comes on, fresh citrus is scarce and the price for a box of limes is sky-high. In January, a case of limes might be twenty dollars; in July, eighty. In January, when the cost of goods is perfect for that classic, dry daiquiri, few tipplers think to order one.

But if we are truly to enjoy a farm-to-glass experience, a reversal, a change in thinking, is needed. Start drinking fresh citrus–driven cocktails in the winter and spirit-filled cocktails in the summer.

The best month to enjoy the freshest daiquiri just might be December, when limes are at their brightest. Imagine you're at your corporate holiday party or you're celebrating Hanukkah or Christmas with the family. It is raining outside, and while everyone else is drinking Scotch on the rocks or big glasses of Cabernet, you order a daiquiri with fresh-squeezed juice from recently harvested limes. Most, if not all, of your family members or colleagues will think you're a nut job. They, along with the barkeep, might bark "What, are you in Tahiti? This ain't Trader Vic's!" But never mind all that. The daiquiri that you've insisted on will be light and bright, with the aroma of the lime at its year-round best. This is true for all cocktails with fresh citrus, especially those that call for lime, which is seemingly every cocktail that originated in Latin America.

# THE
# LEMON DROP

*Given to the world by Henry Africa and beloved
by bachelorettes everywhere*

## LEMON DROP

2 oz/60 ml SKYY citron vodka

1 oz/30 ml fresh lemon juice

1 oz/30 ml Cocktail Syrup (page 59)

3 dashes orange curaçao

Expressed lemon peel for garnish

Pour the liquid into a mixing glass, add ice, shake, then fine-strain
into a cocktail glass and garnish with the lemon peel.

**Henry Africa was on to something. Create a concept that packs the house with ladies and the guys will follow, packing the register with cash.**

After his success with ice-cream daiquiris, Henry turned his attention back to the classic vessel, the cocktail glass, which, as he used to say, "looks lovely in a woman's hand." With a bit of whimsy and a dose of kitsch, Henry unveiled the lemon drop to rousing success. At its core, the drink made quite a bit of sense—it was simply a vodka crusta. The crusta is an old type of sour, before sours needed egg whites. And vodka in the era of Henry Africa was exciting. It was also an empty canvas on which Henry could do his work.

The lemon drop was simple, a bit sweet, and a lot of fun. It quickly spread to saloons across San Francisco. From a flavor perspective, it doesn't fit in with most of San Francisco's favorites; it's bright but barely, and it is neither bitter nor boozy. But, like its younger cousin the Cosmopolitan, it's a rousing success.

I first encountered the lemon drop not as a proper stand-alone cocktail, but as a shooter. When a group of ladies would come to the bar at Wild Ginger, the senior barkeep, Paul Brown, would often suggest a round of lemon drop shots. And if I recall the recipe correctly, it was several of the closest bottles to my hands, which were poured together with a squeeze of lemon. When I met the lemon drop, it had joined the ranks of the purple hooter and the kamikaze. In whatever form it exists, it gets made thousands of times nightly in bars across the country.

To learn many years after the fact that the lemon drop had its origin on San Francisco's Russian Hill was also a lot of fun. As you might imagine, I had to make one for myself. And this is my dirty little secret: The lemon drop recipe I'm sharing with you is rather delicious—a crowd-pleaser, to be sure. (I won't say it's a panty dropper, however. That'd be tacky.) You'll note that the usual rim of sugar has been omitted. As with the margarita in San Francisco that no longer comes with a rim of salt, the crusta and many of its off-spring, having fallen from fashion, no longer include the traditional sugar-lined rim. Nonetheless, I've also made this recipe for plenty of ladies, including my wife, who finds the cocktail delicious. Henry Africa would be pleased.

# SUPERIOR COCKTAIL VODKA

The vodka that Henry Africa preferred in the 1970s would have been very different from most vodka these days. Back then, vodka didn't proclaim to be ultrasmooth and five times distilled; nor did it promise not to give the drinker a hangover. It was the 1970s, damn it, and people were proud of their hangovers.

In those years, producers were not trying to eliminate the spirit's character. Vodka was still entirely associated with Mother Russia and the Eastern Bloc. It was foreign, distilled by Communists on the other side of the Iron Curtain. To think that most vodka brands these days run marketing campaigns that tend toward promoting the removal of flavor, of emasculating the spirit, would have been strange indeed.

My disclaimer for this cocktail vodka is that it isn't entirely made up of just vodka, which is why it works. It is clean and bright while also delivering a bold, spicy flavor. It does not shy away from the palate, yet it is rich with a round, lingering mouthfeel.

## The Bartender's Secret Formula: Superior Cocktail Vodka

24½ oz/700 ml New Amsterdam vodka

7 oz/200 ml Square One organic rye vodka

1¾ oz/50 ml Campo de Encanto Grand & Noble Pisco

1¾ oz/50 ml maraschino liqueur

Blend the liquid into a large vessel, such as a 1-gal/3.8-L pitcher, then allow to rest for 1 week before using.

*Makes 1 qt/1 L*

## Blackberry and Basil Cooler

*By Duggan McDonnell*

3 blackberries

3 or 4 fresh basil leaves

2 oz/60 ml Square One cucumber vodka

1 oz/30 ml fresh lemon juice

½ oz/15 ml diluted agave nectar (see note, page 143)

2 dashes orange bitters

1 oz/30 ml ginger beer

Muddle 2 of the blackberries and the basil leaves in a mixing glass; pour in the vodka, lemon juice, agave nectar, and bitters; add ice; and shake vigorously. Strain into a highball glass over ice while simultaneously pouring in the ginger beer. Garnish with the remaining blackberry.

*Edith Griffin playing piano at the House of Pisco, November 25, 1942*

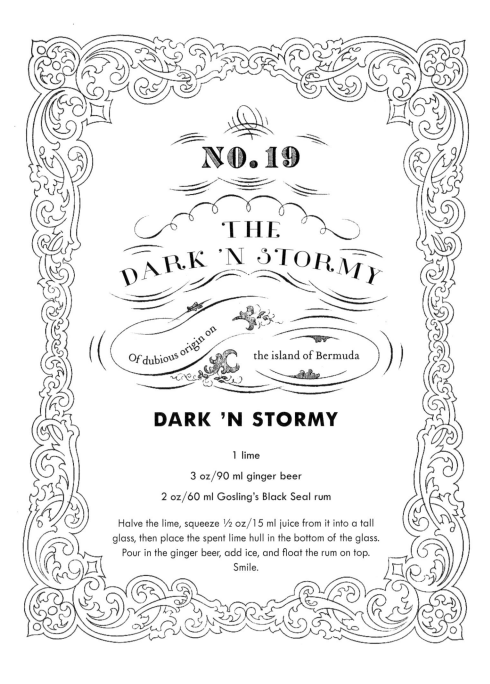

# NO. 19

## THE DARK 'N STORMY

*Of dubious origin on the island of Bermuda*

## DARK 'N STORMY

1 lime

3 oz/90 ml ginger beer

2 oz/60 ml Gosling's Black Seal rum

Halve the lime, squeeze ½ oz/15 ml juice from it into a tall glass, then place the spent lime hull in the bottom of the glass. Pour in the ginger beer, add ice, and float the rum on top. Smile.

On the historic waterfront of San Francisco, amid crumbling old piers, popular museums, and Michelin-starred restaurants, sits a little bar from another era. Inside is a brass-fitted bar top with a tidy, respectable back bar. From its windows you can see the greatest patio in the City, a wooden structure that hangs over the bay and offers views of Treasure Island and of the Oakland Hills to the east. The Blue & Gold commuter ferry chugs northwest past the joint, en route to Pier 39 and then to Sausalito.

This little burg of paradise is the Pier 23 Cafe. The cocktail menu is typically San Franciscan, with a Golden Gate (a smash), a mai tai, a Sazerac, and a Dark 'n Stormy among the listings. On a sunny weekday, the patio is packed with folks who do not keep "regular" working hours or who have perhaps snuck across the street from cubicles inside Levi's Plaza. It's easier to get a tan outside overlooking the bay with a cocktail in hand than inside beneath fluorescent lights.

All around me, folks are drinking their own Dark 'n Stormy, that easy, tall concoction recommended by the barman, though it need not be. In San Francisco, the Dark 'n Stormy sells itself. It is a bold, refreshing cocktail, lightly spiced and effervescent. Originally from Bermuda, the fine folks at Gosling's Black Seal rum attribute its origin to the island's Royal Naval Officers Club and to the ginger beer factory just next door. Much rum was consumed by the Royal Navy, and ginger beer replaced tonic as the popular bubbles of choice; hence, the simplicity of the drink.

But the name is said to have come from the mouth of an old sailor, perhaps a retiree of the Royal Navy, a man who'd had his share of rum in his time, who'd spent many a day beneath sun and moon sailing the high seas. Holding the drink aloft in his hand, he declared it to be the "colour of a cloud only a fool or a dead man would sail under."

Apocryphal or not, that's just the type of cock-tale I love to hear. Rum is a spirit bound to the sea, full of tales of eccentricity and exaggeration. So, too, is San Francisco. Is that why San Franciscans love the Dark 'n Stormy so much?

The style of rum used in the cocktail is often referred to as blackstrap, as extra molasses is blended into it just before bottling. That addition gives the rum a particularly vegetal, rich consistency, which is helpful when floating the spirit atop a drink.

As I finish my second Dark 'n Stormy, I realize its value is a kind of sneak attack: the cocktail is an altogether subtle, easy-to-swill concoction, its buzz overtaking you before you realize it. As the Dark 'n Stormy became more frequently requested in bars across the City, the bottle of Gosling's moved from the back bar down into the speed rail and then, just to make things easier, onto the cocktail menu. Is it the connection to the sea, to the flavor of citrus and lime that made San Francisco embrace the Dark 'n Stormy? I have quizzed many bartenders but have found no consensus on what the connection is. Then again, not all mysteries are meant to be solved.

# SUPERIOR COCKTAIL BLACKSTRAP RUM

Blackstrap rum is delicious, and when blended correctly, has many more uses than the Dark 'n Stormy alone. It can be shaken, stirred, and floated like any other spirit of imagination and integrity.

This superior blend is intentionally more vegetal due to the addition of cachaça from Brazil and overproof rum with a bit of aging on it. It is an aggressive, rewarding blend that is not for the fainthearted. Do not finish the bottle in one sitting!

### The Bartender's Secret Formula: Superior Cocktail Blackstrap Rum

24½ oz/700 ml El Dorado Superior white rum

7 oz/200 ml cachaça, such as Leblon

3½ oz/100 ml Plantation aged overproof rum

1 oz/30 ml blackstrap molasses

1 oz/30 ml Cocktail Syrup (page 59)

Blend the liquid into a large vessel, such as a 1-gal/3.3-L pitcher, then allow to rest for 1 week before using.

*Makes 1 qt/1 L*

*A night view of San Francisco–Oakland Bay Bridge, November 10, 1936*

# GINGER BEER AND SAN FRANCISCO

The City's favorite source of effervescence is, without a doubt, ginger beer, the refresher that comes from the Caribbean and tastes of the Orient. It is full of bubbles, and it can be bitter and sweet. Many brands of ginger beer are available in California, and all of them are freely poured in San Francisco. Here are the three most popular cocktails using this distinctive brew throughout the region.

## Moscow Mule
*Of disputed origin from the City of Angels*

2 oz/60 ml vodka

½ oz/15 ml fresh lime juice

½ oz/15 ml Cocktail Syrup (page 59)

3 oz/90 ml ginger beer

Pour the liquid into a tall glass, add ice, and stir.

## Kentucky Buck
*By Erick Castro, courtesy of Rickhouse*

2 strawberries; 1 sliced for garnish

2 oz/60 ml bourbon

¾ oz/20 ml fresh lemon juice

½ oz/15 ml Cocktail Syrup (page 59)

2 dashes aromatic bitters, homemade (see page 104) or store-bought

2 oz/60 ml ginger beer

Lemon wheel for garnish

Muddle the whole strawberry in a mixing glass, then pour in the bourbon, lemon juice, cocktail syrup, and bitters; shake briefly; and fine-strain into a highball glass over ice while simultaneously pouring in the ginger beer. Garnish with the lemon wheel and sliced strawberry.

## El Diablo
*By Trader Vic Bergeron*

2 oz/60 ml tequila blanco

1 oz/30 ml fresh lime juice

3 oz/90 ml ginger beer

½ oz/15 ml crème de cassis

Pour the tequila, lime juice, and ginger beer into a tall glass, add ice, stir, and float the crème de cassis on top.

# THE BARBARY COAST BARKEEP

*In the time of your life, live—so that in that good
time there shall be no ugliness or death for yourself or for
any life your life touches. Seek goodness everywhere,
and when it is found, bring it out of its hiding
place and let it be free and unashamed.*

*Place in matter and in flesh the least of the values,
for these are the things that hold death and must pass away.
Discover in all things that which shines and is beyond
corruption. Encourage virtue in whatever heart it may
have been driven into secrecy and sorrow by the shame
and terror of the world. Ignore the obvious, for it is
unworthy of the clear eye and the kindly heart.*

*Be the inferior of no man, or of any men be superior.
Remember that every man is a variation of yourself.
No man's guilt is not yours, nor is any man's innocence a
thing apart. Despise evil and ungodliness, but not men of
ungodliness or evil. These, understand. Have no shame in
being kindly and gentle but if the time comes in the time
of your life to kill, kill and have no regret.*

*In the time of your life, live—so that in that wondrous time
you shall not add to the misery and sorrow of the world, but
shall smile to the infinite delight and mystery of it.*

—WILLIAM SAROYAN, *The Time of Your Life*

The DNA of today's barkeep has many traits, from those of the mischievous, conniving entrepreneur "Shanghai" Kelly, who dabbled in drugs, kidnapping, and murder, to those of the more high-minded and pragmatic marketer Duncan Nicol, the culinary innovator Trader Vic, the disciplined Harry Johnson, and the energetic showstoppers, Jerry Thomas and Henry Africa. These six and many more passed along their characteristics to the current generation of barkeeps. And it is when an appealing combination of their traits comes to the fore that we exclaim, "That's a fantastic bartender!"

You might be the type of person who appreciates a bartender who always has a story, a joke ready. You'll find that barkeep in San Francisco. You might like a barkeep who is ever ready to raise a glass and throw back a shot with a guest. You'll find that barkeep in San Francisco. You might be the out-of-town visitor who has come looking for trouble, who always asks the barkeep where the next bar is, who's open later, what corners and alleys hold hidden and sundry delights, and would he or she mind making a few phone calls to turn up that unsavory fun. You'll find that barkeep in San Francisco. You might like to jaw on about sports, the latest contracts signed, and gossip among the various leagues with a barkeep. You'll find that barkeep in San Francisco. You might have just arrived in San Francisco with no plan except that you knew the City was beautiful and that you could easily kill a few days over food and drink, and you want to ask a barkeep for ideas on how you should spend your four-day visit. You'll find that barkeep in San Francisco. You might just want to sit at a bar on your own and have a quiet evening, without actually drinking, and isn't there someone somewhere who understands that, too? You'll find that barkeep in San Francisco. You might want to chat with a barkeep about the nuanced differences between Pinot Gris and Pinot Blanc, or between the terroir of Tuscany and Friuli. You'll find that barkeep in San Francisco. You might suspect that the barkeep in front of you is a master at his or her craft, is a highly knowledgeable repository of fact and fiction on all spirit matters, and can sling a favorite vintage recipe or improvise a fanciful, balanced delight that will calm your day and properly advance your night. You'll most definitely find that barkeep in San Francisco.

Here in California, the barkeep is especially endowed with that sense of Western bravado, that can-do energy that kicks life along. There's a fearless sense of opportunism blended with a desire for the finer things in life. It's an attitude, a state of mind that can lead to vice but, in the end, is an absolute virtue in a barkeep. In more than a decade of tending bar in San Francisco's Union Square, I have experienced every example in the preceding paragraph, often within a single night, often night after night. A great barkeep is an amorphous beast, full of talent and pluck and always ready to engage the public. From guest to guest and night to night, the needs of the public change, and it's the great barkeep who understands and embraces the situation. More than improvisation in the cocktail tin is required. The barkeep must employ psychology and intuition and maintain a calm bar-side manner and nerves of steel, all the while continuing to shake and send forth drinks across the wood. And when that happens, again we exclaim, "That's a fantastic bartender!"

I wrote previously that the January 2006 issue of *Food & Wine* magazine published a cover story in which I was featured as a leader of the American cocktail revolution. Was I really a leader? I wondered. And am I also another link in the long line of great barkeeps in San Francisco, an eighth-generation mixologist eager to pass on the torch when time dictates?

In the summer of 2003, I stepped behind the bar at Harry Denton's Starlight Room and worked cheek by jowl shaking and stirring with Marco Dionysos, who at the time was the City's most notorious mixologist. We both wore tuxedos and we toiled furiously. The harder I worked to deliver quality-driven cocktails consistently and fast amid the bawdy glamour of the Starlight Room, the more I admired Harry. He was vibrant, a regal visionary who held court while also wearing a tuxedo, though he was far less sweaty. Harry had spent decades running high-end saloons in San Francisco since first tending bar alongside his mentor, Henry Africa, at Henry's eponymous saloon in 1971. Henry, who had been known as Norman Hobday by his mother and father, had been highly influenced by fellow San Franciscan Trader Vic Bergeron, by his aesthetic of escapism and his flamboyant, fresh cocktails, not to mention his crafting of a new identity. Henry was famous for his many-flavored daiquiris, but his legacy remains the lemon drop. Trader Vic had come of age during Prohibition, and it was in 1934, just as the sun set on the Noble Experiment (and a few years after the death of Duncan Nicol) that the Trader set his imagination alive as a restaurateur. Vic was absolutely committed to delivering an outlandish, highly innovative experience inspired by the flavors of the Pacific.

But, like all of us, Vic began by promoting and delivering the prized cocktails of his mentors, including Duncan Nicol's South American delight, the Pisco punch, on his first cocktail menu. Nicol spent the better part of his life on Montgomery Street in the Bank Exchange Saloon, fulfilling many a barkeep's dream of buying the bar he had worked in every day. In 1893, with the place in his name, he perfected and promoted the culture of punches with Pisco at the Bank Exchange, trimming the offerings to one singular concoction of perfection until the saloon was shuttered in 1919. This was a tremendous feat, as competition was fierce in Nicol's, or should I say "Cocktail Bill" Boothby's, era. Boothby, who had published his *Cocktail Boothby's American Bar-Tender* in 1891, was a flamboyant minstrel-cum-barman who dubbed himself Presiding Deity over the bar. He was like his ancestors and all of his descendants already named: an ambitious character, a virtuoso, a local celebrity. He had emerged as a barman after studying the books of two local legends: Jerry Thomas's *How to Mix Drinks, or The Bon-Vivant's Companion* and Harry Johnson's *New and Improved Bartenders' Manual.*

Jerry Thomas had stood successfully behind the redwood bars on San Francisco's first town plaza, Portsmouth Square, and Harry Johnson, who was of German ancestry, was a meticulous, imaginative barman who had created dozens of cocktail recipes. Although the two men shared a profession, they were very different. Johnson was a master mechanic, his behavior pure and reputation impeccable, qualities that set him apart from the denizens of the Devil's Acre. Perhaps his character was preordained by his German

American background, or maybe it was a conscious reaction to the bold, bombastic Jerry Thomas. Thomas was San Francisco's first barman impresario whose audacious persona overshadowed his greatest culinary feat: merely igniting alcohol and pouring it from glass to glass. He had been the life of the party from the moment he stepped behind a bar in San Francisco in 1849, having perfectly understood the idea of the bar as a stage. San Francisco was growing rapidly and needed entertainment, and Jerry Thomas provided it. And the best barkeeps today do as well. A direct ancestral line runs from the City's contemporary barkeeps, from myself back to the beginning of time, so to speak, to 1849 when Portsmouth Square was the Garden of Eden and civilization was beginning to blossom in San Francisco.

"It is related that once, when a gang of desperadoes swarmed into the El Dorado intent upon robbery, the Professor suavely suggested that they refresh themselves before proceeding with their enterprise," Herbert Asbury wrote of Jerry Thomas in an introduction to a 1920s edition of *How to Mix Drinks*. "They assented, whereupon he prepared a dram which stretched them quivering and helpless upon the floor. The Vigilantes then hanged them with considerable ceremony." Capable, charming, steadfast, and direct, a liquid chef from the very first man, these are the traits of a barkeep passed down the family tree since Abraham, er, Jerry blazed the path so long ago.

As I look back on these lives, on the eight generations that came before me, I see the outright bluster and the impassioned craft of Denton, Hobday, Bergeron, Nicol, Boothby, Johnson, and then Thomas, and from this tapestry a bold portrait emerges. It is like looking into a mirror. Through them I come to recognize myself, there along the sagging jawline, among the cracks and crevices of truth wrought by laughter, by too much drink, and by many, many late nights. There I see a barman, pedigreed and awaiting his progeny, a face for the next generation.

# THE GINGER ROGERS

*Created by Marcovaldo Dionysos to
lead the cocktail renaissance*

## GINGER ROGERS

10 to 12 fresh mint leaves, plus 1 sprig for garnish

2 oz/60 ml London dry gin

¾ oz/20 ml fresh lemon juice

¾ oz/20 ml ginger syrup

2 oz/60 ml ginger ale

Muddle the mint leaves in a highball glass, then pour
in the liquid, add ice, and stir. Garnish with the mint
sprig and sip away.

The most interesting thing about Marcovaldo Dionysos isn't his name. It's his utter dedication and consummate passion for the craft of the cocktail. Marco has worked at nearly all of the influential cocktail programs in San Francisco of the past twenty years, and the few that he missed is where you would find him after a shift, enjoying a cocktail or three.

Marco gave San Francisco an enduring legacy in the form of several cocktails, including the superb Ginger Rogers, but it was his dedication that made the bartenders of San Francisco better. More than ten years ago, long before he migrated north to the Rose City to open Teardrop Lounge, Daniel Shoemaker quipped to me, "I'm just sick of everyone saying that Marco is the best bartender in San Francisco." Daniel wasn't being resentful; he was, and is, a logical, even-tempered, and ambitious fellow. And he wasn't exaggerating, either.

For an era, it was largely agreed that Mr. Dionysos was the best barkeep in San Francisco, which also meant that he was among the best in all the land, if not the world. The majority of recipes in this book originated with barmen over the age of forty who came up alongside, or shall we say, beneath the career of Marco. Many of the bartenders I have named in these pages have contributed extraordinary things to the cocktail culture of San Francisco, as bar managers, owners, consultants, and authors, and all will readily note the talent of Marco. The most sincere will also admit that to be as good as, if not better than, Marco motivated them.

If you're reading this book, it's because you love a great cocktail and have experienced that in San Francisco. There have been many City bartenders who were motivated to be better, to deliver smarter, fresher cocktail programs because of Marco, including yours truly.

When I worked alongside Marco in the summer of 2003 at the Starlight Room, I could not keep up with his talent. I was the boy in the company of a man, and I had no business shaking and stirring behind the same bar.

Later, I worked at Absinthe Brasserie & Bar, where the Ginger Rogers had made its San Francisco debut in 1998. It was the most popular drink on the menu, and although it was fairly simple, it seemed to inspire and revitalize the community. But every new drink I created, every new menu I wrote, there was Marco as a little devil on my shoulder, ever a monkey on my back. How did my work compare with the very best?

On paper, the Ginger Rogers reads like a gin-crossed Moscow mule that got mixed up with a mojito. It is an aromatic cocktail in which the citrus, ginger, and mint work wonderfully together. Now, rewind to 1998 and recall the anti-mojito era; also keep in mind that vodka was reigning supreme at the time. Here was a cocktail, the top-selling cocktail of the joint, that was gin-based and required a fair bit of labor to boot. In 1998, Americans were once again starting to figure out gin. And if San Francisco was the hub of the cocktail renaissance, we can trace a point of origin to the Absinthe bar with Marco Dionysos in 1998.

I asked Marco to recall that era. "The dot-com era was a new gold rush," he told me. "All that disposable income fueled the cocktail revival. But I also believe it was driven by bartenders. There was a new pool of customers who had money to spend and were eager to upgrade their drinking habits. I worked briefly at Stars, and I was struck by how old money was resistant to try new things. They assumed they were the arbiters of what was good and they stuck to their choices of vodka, Scotch, or whatever. The dot-com crowd was like the nouveau riche of the gold rush and eager to try new things. Over at Absinthe, just a few blocks away, I was exhuming old cocktails to match the fin de siècle concept of the bar, and the geekiness of the menu appealed to the geekiness of the dot-commers." Was it kismet or just history repeating itself in San Francisco?

When you make a Ginger Rogers, remember the steps are exactly the same as for a mojito, but the result just might be a little more complex.

# NO. 21

## THE BLOOD AND SAND

*Published by Harry Craddock of the old Savoy Hotel, London, and
reinvigorated by a new generation of Fog City barkeeps*

## BLOOD AND SAND

¾ oz/20 ml blended Scotch, such as Great King Street

¾ oz/20 ml Heering cherry liqueur

¾ oz/20 ml Italian vermouth

¾ oz/20 ml fresh orange juice

Expressed orange peel for garnish

Pour the liquid into a mixing glass, add ice, shake briefly,
then fine-strain into a cocktail glass. Garnish with the orange
peel and wink at your neighbor.

Back at the Comstock Saloon, the cocktail known as the Blood and Sand is prepared in a flash, with the same speed that a night-club barkeep uses to grab multiple bottles all at once, pouring equal portions, and then, after a quick shake, the masterpiece is slid across the wood.

It is an obscure cocktail of unknown origin that first appeared in an old British cocktail book. An orphan, it also has the wildest ingredients in equal parts: Scotch, Heering cherry liqueur, Italian vermouth, and orange juice. Like Rob Roy in drag. At least somebody thought to give this bamboozle a tough-sounding name, otherwise not one of us would have bothered with it.

But here's the catch: the Blood and Sand is a resounding success in a way that never fails to amaze. The ingredients simply shouldn't work together, yet they do. Bartenders are dumbfounded by the drink. They simply have to keep making it. It has long been an incredibly popular tipple throughout the City. Plus, place a Blood and Sand on a cocktail menu and you'll be getting a thank-you note from the fine folks who produce the unique Heering liqueur.

The Blood and Sand is delicious and a crowd-pleaser for both sexes. Somehow the result of the strange recipe is perfectly balanced. And this explains why the dame behind-the-stick on Columbus Avenue can shake them with abandon. "No one ever sends them back," Karri Cormican told me.

Why can't it always be that simple?

# ON COCKTAILS
# WITH EQUAL PROPORTIONS

The Blood and Sand, like the Negroni, is a cocktail composed of seemingly disparate elements that, when poured together in equal amounts, create a surprisingly good drink. There are others like this, cocktails slung from recipes without a hierarchy, where the sum is much greater than the parts. The last word is one. It's got a resounding title, but who's really in charge? Who's holding the figurative conch? No one! And yet, peacefully, the four soldiers in the last word come to a mighty accord.

Others of similar construction include the corpse reviver cocktail, the Barbary Coast, even the Vieux Carré. When you read the recipes for each of these, you think to yourself, Somebody got it all wrong. As it turns out, cocktails composed from ingredients measured out in equal parts aren't such a bad thing, which is why I'm back at Comstock Saloon, hoping for another Blood and Sand.

*U. C. Stephen Union Tap Room, March 23, 1933*

## Last Word

*Courtesy of Zig Zag Café, Seattle*

¾ oz/20 ml gin

¾ oz/20 ml maraschino liqueur

¾ oz/20 ml green Chartreuse

¾ oz/20 ml fresh lime juice

Pour the liquid into a mixing glass, add ice, shake, then strain into a cocktail glass.

## Corpse Reviver #2

*Of unknown origin*

¾ oz/20 ml gin

¾ oz/20 ml orange curaçao

¾ oz/20 ml Lillet Blanc or Jardesca California aperitif wine

¾ oz/20 ml fresh lemon juice

3 dashes absinthe

Pour the liquid into a mixing glass, add ice, shake, then strain into a cocktail glass.

## Barbary Coast

*Of unknown origin*

¾ oz/20 ml blended Scotch, such as Dewar's or Famous Grouse

¾ oz/20 ml gin

¾ oz/20 ml crème de cacao

¾ oz/20 ml heavy cream

Dusting of ground nutmeg for garnish

Pour the liquid into a mixing glass, add ice, shake, then fine-strain into a cocktail glass and garnish with the nutmeg.

# THE
# SANGRIA

*Created by Harry Johnson, just like so many other cocktails*

## SANGRIA

3 oz/90 ml California red wine

1 oz/30 ml fresh orange juice

1 oz/30 ml fresh lime juice

1 oz/30 ml Chinese Five-Spice Agave Nectar (page 148)

½ oz/15 ml California brandy

½ oz/15 ml aged rum

½ oz/15 ml Punt e Mes

3 dashes Bénédictine D.O.M.

1 oz/30 ml seltzer

Fresh fruit of choice for garnish

Pour the wine, citrus juices, agave nectar, brandy, rum, Punt e Mes, and Bénédictine into a mixing glass, add ice, then shake briefly. Strain into a tall punch glass over ice while simultaneously pouring in the seltzer. Garnish with fruit *y sonreírse*!

Sangria gets no respect. It is roundly thought of as the drink that only the cheapest ingredients go into making. Can you imagine a completely different sangria, one composed of a Super Tuscan Cabernet, V.S.O.P. Cognac, farmers' market fresh fruit, and just a little locally produced honey to sweeten it? It would sell like hot cakes! Premium ingredients always make better cocktails, no matter the type of cocktail.

Using wine in cocktails is considered by some to be parochial, something reserved for backyard mixology. That too is a shame.

California is the home of wine production in the United States, and since the days of the Barbary Coast, wine, whether fortified, aromatized, sparkling, or still, has had a place in mixology. In fact, the word *sangria* is relatively new to our shores, having come from Spain and rising in popularity only since World War II. In nineteenth-century San Francisco, port wine punch, the Champagne cobbler, the St. Charles punch, the mullet claret, the sherry cobbler, and the vermouth cocktail, among many others, all called for some form of wine. That long tradition of wine in mixology has gone unrealized by many, or maybe the tradition is so common that it has been taken for granted.

Sangria itself is eerily reminiscent of many of the wine and brandy punches listed in Harry Johnson's *New and Improved Bartender's Manual*. No matter. This book has proven that many great cocktails have their roots here, or perhaps, like collective consciousness, inventions of a similar sort happened in different places at the same time. Sangria, then, is emblematic of the historic cocktail in San Francisco, of the City's Spanish roots and her ongoing partiality for adding a little wine to many a cocktail.

# SUPERIOR COCKTAIL FRENCH VERMOUTH

This vermouth blend is exciting and was inspired entirely by vermouth of yesteryear: bold, rich, fruit-driven, oxidized concoctions that were darker in color and added a stronger dimension to cocktails.

Based on nimble dry Riesling from the United States, the blend starts lean and bright and then receives layers of aromas, herbs, and mouthfeel from white vermouth, sherry, and Pineau des Charentes. Both the sherry and the Pineau des Charentes should be slightly oxidized, yet stable; these Old World characteristics meld perfectly with the light and bright Riesling. In addition, most of the flavor of this vermouth comes from the grapes themselves, rather than herbs macerated or distilled, as only 20 percent of the blend is sourced from commercial vermouth.

Not only will this blend renew your vigor for vermouth mixology, but you'll likely sip it on its own, over ice, with seltzer, with tonic, with a slice of cucumber—until the bottle is gone. That's how good dry vermouth can, and should, be.

## The Bartender's Secret Formula: Superior Cocktail French Vermouth

24½ oz/700 ml dry Riesling

7 oz/200 ml bianco (sweet white) vermouth, such as Martini or Cinzano

1¾ oz/50 ml amontillado sherry

1¾ oz/50 ml aged Pineau des Charentes

Blend the liquid into a large vessel, such as a 1-gal/3.8-L pitcher, then allow to rest for 1 week before using.

*Makes 1 qt/1 L*

## Intermezzo

*By Duggan McDonnell*

3 or 4 fresh basil leaves

3 oz/90 ml Jardesca California aperitif wine

½ oz/15 ml fresh lemon juice

½ oz/15 ml Cocktail Syrup (page 59)

2 dashes orange bitters

2 oz/60 ml seltzer

Thin cucumber slice for garnish

Muddle the basil leaves in a tall glass, then pour in the liquid. Fill the glass with ice, stir, and garnish with the cucumber slice.

## Dr. T

*By Jacques Bezuidenhout, courtesy of the Starlight Room*

1 egg white

1½ oz/45 ml Partida tequila blanco

1½ oz/45 ml dry Riesling

½ oz/15 ml fresh lemon juice

½ oz/15 ml Cocktail Syrup (page 59)

¼ oz/10 ml Islay Scotch whisky

Pour the liquid into a mixing glass, add ice, shake, then fine-strain into a cocktail glass.

## Bamboo Cocktail

*By Louis Eppinger or "Cocktail Bill" Boothby*

2 oz/60 ml fino sherry

1 oz/30 ml French vermouth

2 dashes orange bitters

2 dashes aromatic bitters, homemade (see page 104) or store-bought

Expressed orange peel for garnish

Pour the liquid into a mixing glass, add ice, stir forty times, then strain into a cocktail coupe and garnish with the orange peel.

# HETCH HETCHY'S PURE WATER AND THE ICE IN EVERY SAN FRANCISCAN COCKTAIL

❦

*The champion, the unsung hero of every cocktail slung in San Francisco, is John Muir's Yosemite National Park and its Hetch Hetchy Reservoir, the source of the City's water.*

In the past fifteen years, a worldwide renaissance has taken place in which people have begun to give a damn about the ice used in the making and serving of cocktails. Bars and restaurants have gone to the great expense of purchasing several different ice machines in order to offer hand-carved ice spheres, have acquired an on-site chainsaw for cutting large blocks of ice, and have shaken some cocktails without any ice at all and then poured the dram over crushed, shaved, or cracked ice or just a single frozen stone. Such changes have yielded some amazing aesthetic differences and have made the preparation and presentation of cocktails that much more thought provoking. But by heightening the style of the ice has the substance of the ice been overlooked?

The champion, the unsung hero of every cocktail slung in San Francisco, is John Muir's Yosemite National Park and its Hetch Hetchy Reservoir, the source of the City's water. Ice is the quintessential, indispensible ingredient in every cocktail, if not the largest ingredient by liquid volume. It is used in the stirring, shaking, and smashing of nearly every cocktail and is then used to hold the structure and temperature of, say, a margarita after it is poured tall in the glass.

No matter the shape of the ice cube used in making a margarita or a pitcher of backyard sangria in San Francisco, it is the source of the water that matters most. And the Hetch Hetchy Reservoir is revered as having some of the purest drinking water in the world. Other cities of note have fantastic drinking water, such as Portland, Oregon, and New York City, but such well-known drinking outposts as Las Vegas, San Diego, and even beautiful Honolulu have all received low ratings from agencies that survey the quality of drinking water. Where so many cocktails are shaken, the water deserves to be better.

Can the difference be tasted in a cocktail? Absolutely. In cocktails prepared with wine, which typically have a lower alcohol level, ice will influence the flavor of the drink even more, as there is less alcohol to be diluted.

As a barman, I have long been a champion of better, cleaner drinking water. I have to be. In a sense, Hetch Hetchy has always been my business partner. Without her steady, pure supply, every cocktail served in San Francisco wouldn't be the same. Her water is an undeniable part of our terroir, our story, and is one of the reasons why cocktails can be so damn delicious in Fog City. Knowing how fortunate cocktail drinkers in San Francisco are has found me encouraging barkeeps across the country to learn more about their water source and, if necessary, to advocate for a better water supply, if only to deliver their best work in the glass.

*View across Hetch Hetchy Valley, early 1900s*

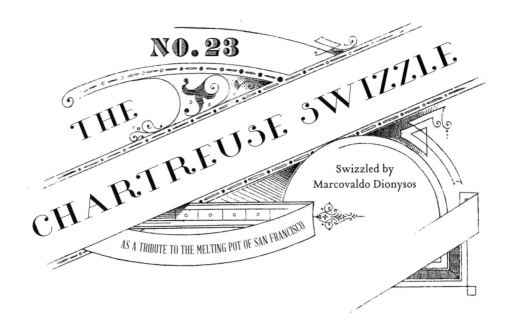

NO. 23

THE CHARTREUSE SWIZZLE

Swizzled by
Marcovaldo Dionysos

AS A TRIBUTE TO THE MELTING POT OF SAN FRANCISCO

## CHARTREUSE SWIZZLE

1¼ oz/35 ml green Chartreuse

1 oz/30 ml pineapple juice

½ oz/15 ml fresh lime juice

½ oz/15 ml Velvet Falernum liqueur

Lime wheel for garnish

Pour the liquid into a tall glass and agitate heartily with either a bar
spoon or a proper swizzle stick. Fill with crushed ice,
garnish with the lime wheel, and smile.

The very first time I tasted the mystic herbal liqueur compounded by Carthusian monks was above the clouds in the Starlight Room. Fear rose in my throat as the barkeep poured three fingers of the dark green liqueur. "Bottoms up," toasted Erik Carlson, friend and colleague from MECCA, who has since become one of Seattle's best barmen. His glass hit the bar top before mine and then what he said next caused me to choke. "We'll have another."

The Chartreuse lingered in my mouth, traveled down my throat, and expanded in my chest. It wasn't at all what I was expecting. It was delicious, magical, potent stuff. And after two shots, I was hammered. The moral of the story is that Chartreuse, that high-proof noble liqueur, delivers an exquisite performance when employed in adequate doses. Several cocktail recipes in this book call for Chartreuse, chief among them Marco Dionysos's dynamic Chartreuse swizzle.

The term *swizzle* is used for a long drink that calls for a swizzle stick, an almost prehistoric bar tool—literally, a stick—that fans out at its base with four sections. It looks like a tiny upside-down coat rack. You place the coat rack amid the liquid and ice in the base of your glass and swizzle away. The technique and its tool were invented in rural parts of the Caribbean long before tin cups and Boston shakers came to dominate.

The Chartreuse swizzle is a masterful combination. Lime and pineapple always play well together, as do the additional baking spices from the Falernum. Layer in the more than one hundred herbs and spices blended into Chartreuse and its round base of French brandy and you've got an exquisitely bright, boozy cocktail. That's why the Chartreuse swizzle has been picked up and poached onto cocktail menus across the City and across the country.

It seems like a new cocktail, a bit avant-garde at first. But remember that San Francisco received more than thirty thousand French immigrants in its first decade, and they brought with them Chartreuse and every other liqueur they could from France. Plenty of other folks from around the world were showing up at the same time and bringing their liqueurs, including the spices and tastes of the Caribbean. Early San Francisco was a melting pot, and the Chartreuse swizzle embodies that tradition.

The other tradition carried on here is that Marcovaldo Dionysos wasn't born with that name. And having reached this point in the book, you know that adopting a new moniker is a long and cherished tradition among San Francisco's barmen.

*Sir Francis Drake Hotel, 1937*

# ON USING A LIQUEUR
# AS A PRINCIPAL SPIRIT

A liqueur is most often thought of as something to sip by itself or to drizzle into a cocktail. Due to their sugar content, or just plain fruitiness, liqueurs are relegated to playing second fiddle.

That needn't be the case, and the Chartreuse swizzle, which has two liqueurs in its composition, proves that. Think about Pimm's, Cointreau, even the many amari embraced in San Francisco; each has its place and can rightfully assume the leadership role in any cocktail. The trick is getting the balance of alcohol, acid, and sugar just right.

## Midnight Smash
*By Duggan McDonnell*

4 blackberries

1 oz/30 ml Averna

1 oz/30 ml Charbay blood orange vodka

1 oz/30 ml fresh Meyer lemon juice

2 oz/60 ml ginger beer

Orange wheel for garnish

Muddle 3 of the blackberries in a mixing glass, then pour in the Averna, vodka, and lemon juice and add ice. Shake vigorously, then strain into a tall glass filled with ice while simultaneously pouring in the ginger beer. Garnish with the orange wheel and remaining blackberry.

## Pimm's Cup
*Of unknown orgin*

2 oz/60 ml Pimm's No. 1

½ oz/15 ml fresh lemon juice

½ oz/15 ml ginger syrup

3 oz/90 ml lemon-lime soda

Thin cucumber slice, lemon slice, and fresh mint sprig for garnish

Pour the liquid into a tall glass, add ice, stir, and garnish with the cucumber and lemon slices and the mint sprig.

# THE BASIL GIMLET

*Muddled and shaken by Greg Lindgren, Carl Christiansen, and the Heart of the City Farmers' Market*

## BASIL GIMLET

5 fresh basil leaves, plus 1 sprig for garnish

2 oz/60 ml Junipero gin

1 oz/30 ml fresh lime juice

½ oz/15 ml Cocktail Syrup (page 59)

Lemon wheel for garnish

Muddle the basil leaves in a mixing glass, then pour in the liquid, add ice, and shake vigorously. Fine-strain into a cocktail glass, garnish with either the lemon wheel or sprig of basil, and inhale the aroma.

In 2008, the basil gimlet arrived as the drink of the summer. It had appeared for the first time in San Francisco in 2006, on a menu at Rye, a tiny bar at the northern edge of the Tenderloin. Two years later, guests would enter Cantina and order a basil gimlet as if it was a known commodity, like a Moscow mule or a Pimm's cup. I knew the basil gimlet because I was a fan of Rye; I'd enjoyed one inside its modern walls. On one occasion when a guest called for the savory refresher, I also learned a lesson in service.

"Basil gimlet, please," the quick exchange began.

"We don't have that drink on our menu," I protested.

"But you can make it, right?" came the guest's reply, flat and certain of what she wanted.

The basil gimlet had reached critical mass. The crowd that ordered it might have been the same crowd to have ordered the lemon drop or the mojito in a previous life, who now ordered the Ginger Rogers and the Laughing Buddha. The basil gimlet was bright, delicious, somewhat disarming. When I asked the guest if she preferred vodka or gin in her gimlet, she replied, "Does it matter?"

I knew the answer. I had asked Greg Lindgren, a partner in Rye, how the phenomenon of the basil gimlet came to be, to which he replied, "We had just opened Rye and were so busy with everything else, we hadn't yet created a cocktail menu. Shelley [his wife and a famed restaurateur] called from Boston to check in and told me that she'd just had dinner at Carl Christiansen's new restaurant and enjoyed the most amazing basil gimlets." I knew Carl well, as he had hired me for my first job tending bar in San Francisco at his former restaurant, MECCA.

"'Well, what's in it?' I asked her," Greg continued.

"Basil and gimlet?" I retorted.

"Exactly. So, we just made up our own recipe and it took off."

Yeah, it did. Carl Christiansen had always been a very attentive restaurateur who, while running MECCA, exercised a strong hand over the bar and its cocktail program, never a detail missed. I wondered if the same thing was happening out in Beantown.

In a very short time, the basil gimlet has come to be considered a modern classic. It has appeared in many national media outlets and has been appropriated by menus around the country, most notably at Las Vegas's Bellagio.

## Carmen Amaya

*By Jordan Mackay, courtesy of Cantina*

4 fresh basil leaves

1½ oz/45 ml rye whiskey

½ oz/15 ml rich amontillado sherry

½ oz/15 ml Cointreau

1 oz/30 ml fresh lemon juice

½ oz/15 ml Cocktail Syrup (page 59)

2 dashes orange bitters

Expressed orange peel for garnish

Muddle the basil leaves and 3 ice cubes in a mixing glass, smashing them together, then pour in the liquid, add additional ice, and shake vigorously. Fine-strain into a cocktail glass and garnish with the orange peel.

*Bartender standing in unidentified bar, n.d.*

# THE HANDS THAT TASTE

*If you put a sprig of rosemary under your nose you will quickly recognize its general odor and you will note that it's rosemary. But you can also take a few moments to dissect the various compounds of its general fragrance and thus discover that rosemary contains wood, floral and spice tones as well as notes of camphor and euca-lyptus. That's the difference between "smelling" and "experiencing," between "drinking" and "savoring."*

—François Chartier, *Taste Buds and Molecules: The Art of Science, Food and Flavor*

To every barkeep I've had the pleasure of hiring and to the students of every cocktail class I teach, I proclaim one universal truth: The most important tool used in cocktail making is neither the shaker nor the strainer, it isn't the bar spoon or the wooden pestle. The most important tool for every bartender is a tasting straw.

Organoleptic evaluation is an essential aspect in cocktail making, so you must taste any and every cocktail before you serve it. No matter the ingredients, the recipe, the method of preparation, or how many times you have made the same basil gimlet, before straining the glory from the tin, you must pop in a straw, cover one opening with your forefinger, and then remove your finger once the other end is in your mouth, thus releasing a petite taste for your analysis. Every now and then something will have changed, and the recipe will need a minor adjustment. This is the only way to discover that, to ensure that, perfect, balanced cocktail.

I began this practice very early in my career, and as I developed, I was constantly adjusting drinks to arrive at a seamless bright balance. I anchored the ritual with a continual tasting of every bottle on the back bar, of fresh lime juice at room temperature, of bitters licked off the back of my hand, of cracked peppercorns and fresh basil. And I committed all of it to memory. Between my nose and my tongue, my head and my hands, I accrued hundreds, if not thousands, of flavor combinations that I'd experienced, created, and then knew exactly what would happen should an adjustment be needed, an extra ingredient added, a step taken away. Imagine then on a heated Saturday night, with hip-hop and R&B playing just a bit too loudly and the crowd at the bar three people deep waiting to order a fresh cocktail, how quickly my tongue must process every bit of information that has gone up to my brain from the tasting straw and then down to my hands as they reach for bottle after bottle. In the middle of making every cocktail, it is as if I am tasting every ingredient.

If I grab a bottle of rye whiskey, my mind tells my hand exactly what my tongue once tasted. During the three seconds that it takes me to grab and then pour the rye, the spiced, robust experience of rye washes over my palate. You see, I have developed a kinetic palate; a physical interface with my tongue as the portal and my hands as the outgoing arbiters of experience. My hands are able to pour what information they receive at a moment's notice, improvise as needed, with the next bottle changing the virtual and real chemistry in my mind and in the glass simultaneously. I will shake the drink at length if it is similar to a Caipirinha or a Pisco sour, and give it only a brief whirl if it resembles a last word or a Blood and Sand.

Imagine then, above the din of the deejay, when one of those guests who has been waiting for a fresh cocktail simply shouts, "Just make me something different!" I can choose to be annoyed, deflect her order, and demand that she be more specific. Or I can be compassion-ate in that moment knowing that I have trained myself for times like this, and that my guest has money in her hand and only wants one of my delicious drinks to sip while she dances to hip-hop and R&B. On the many thousands of occasions that this has happened,

I have always chosen to take thirty seconds and, using all of what I know of cocktails and of the guest just in front of me, I'll shake up a cocktail just for her, before moving on to sell another drink to the next guest already waiting.

This practice of constant organoleptic evaluation is not only a means to ensure that every cocktail is balanced before serving but also a way to educate and enrich your memory bank, keeping your kinetic palate sharp. In the case of the Carmen Amaya (see page 227), for example, I'll smack the leaves of basil in my hand before dropping them into the mixing glass. The savory scent fills the air as I set a few ice cubes in the glass. When I smash the cubes and leaves together, creating a hand-crushed ice full of beautiful green flecks, I know exactly what that chilled, diluted basil ice tastes like. I then pour in the heavy, spiced rye whiskey, followed by the lemon juice, to create a tart, savory, bitter, and boozy slush. The drink is still incomplete, which is why the recipe calls for Cointreau, amontillado sherry, and cocktail syrup, from which we get the flavors of orange and that almond-driven mouthfeel along with a profound sweetness. Add a dash of orange bitters and shake just longer than you'd think necessary, and the Carmen Amaya, like her namesake, will dance on your tongue, back and forth, filling out your palate and splashing down your gullet. To truly know what a cocktail is like, why it works the way it does, is to know its every step.

This is why the simple plastic straw used to taste every cocktail is the barkeep's best friend, the most important tool behind every bar.

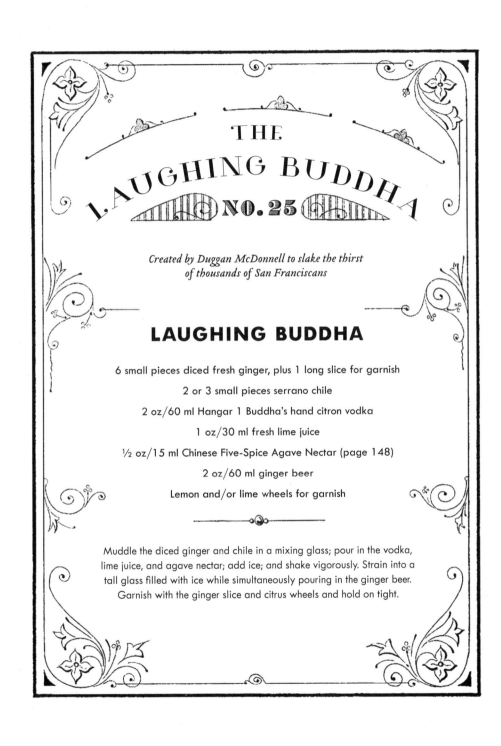

# THE LAUGHING BUDDHA NO. 25

*Created by Duggan McDonnell to slake the thirst
of thousands of San Franciscans*

## LAUGHING BUDDHA

6 small pieces diced fresh ginger, plus 1 long slice for garnish

2 or 3 small pieces serrano chile

2 oz/60 ml Hangar 1 Buddha's hand citron vodka

1 oz/30 ml fresh lime juice

½ oz/15 ml Chinese Five-Spice Agave Nectar (page 148)

2 oz/60 ml ginger beer

Lemon and/or lime wheels for garnish

Muddle the diced ginger and chile in a mixing glass; pour in the vodka,
lime juice, and agave nectar; add ice; and shake vigorously. Strain into a
tall glass filled with ice while simultaneously pouring in the ginger beer.
Garnish with the ginger slice and citrus wheels and hold on tight.

Years before the fine folks at Yelp informed me that the Laughing Buddha served at Cantina was the signature cocktail most mentioned on the site, I had an idea of its popularity. Was it the many cases of citron vodka being emptied every week, the constant muddling of ginger with chiles, or the fact that at some point people stopped reading the menu and instead just sat down and said, "Two Laughing Buddhas, please"?

It was all of these. The drink came about in an odd sort of way. It was a sunny spring afternoon and I was sitting in Alamo Square Park overlooking the "painted ladies" and their view of San Francisco. I was snacking on a bag of Spicy Thai Kettle Chips, very much enjoying their flavor, when I thought to myself. *This would make an amazing cocktail.* I flipped the bag and read the ingredients: chiles, ginger, honey, citrus, and spices. Wow!

With inspiration percolating, I set about its construction. This is the cocktail for which I created Chinese Five-Spice Agave Nectar (page 148). When I finished, I knew that the cooler was a good quick fix, but I never guessed that it would work so well.

The name of the cocktail was conjured from the many portly Buddhas in the shop windows of Chinatown. The little red statuettes of the heavyset and happy god with the long earlobes always seemed to offer a blessing. I hoped the Laughing Buddha would do the same for San Francisco.

This cocktail is of distinctly San Francisco origin. Beyond the principal spirit originating locally, it brings together the flavors of the East and the West: ginger from the Orient and chiles from Mexico; agave nectar also from Mexico and a five-spice delight from China. It is a tall drink similar in construction to the Dark 'n Stormy, the Kentucky buck, and to California's own, the Moscow mule. It is a muddled cocktail, which Mr. Mojito also made so well when he tended bar at Cantina. It is a balanced, yet heartily spiced, bright delight, with a hint of vegetal bitterness and nearly two shots of booze to make its construction authentic.

One night in spring 2008, as I was tending bar to a packed Thursday evening crowd, I chatted across the wood with one of my regulars, Felicia Sanchez. She was sipping on a Laughing Buddha, and as she spoke, she coyly nibbled at the end of her straw. "You know what this drink tastes like?" she asked me.

"Tell me," I replied.

"Those bags of spicy Thai chips!" No one had or has since voiced that connection, that little inspiration, to me. I was tickled.

"Come with me," I said. When she asked where we were going, I told that we were going to the market to buy some chips.

As I rushed out with Felicia at my side in search of a bag of Spicy Thai Kettle Chips, I left the only other barkeep to tend to the horde on her own. When we tell people how we met, we divulge that we did meet in a bar, a particular bar, and that for our first date we went to Walgreens. It wasn't long after, full of the pluck of my persona, that I said to myself, I'm gonna marry that gal!

Will the Laughing Buddha also live on, a cocktail indicative of San Francisco and embraced by the next generation? Perhaps. It was served at our wedding.

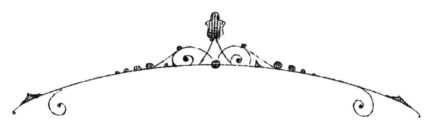

# TO CREATE EVERY COCKTAIL
# WITH LOVE

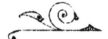 

*It seems to me that our three basic needs,
for food and security and love, are so mixed and
mingled and entwined that we cannot straightly
think of one without the others. So it happens
when I write of hunger, I am really writing about
love and the hunger for it, and warmth and the
love of it and the hunger for it.*

—M. F. K. FISHER, *The Gastronomical Me*

Craig Claiborne said it best, "Cooking is at once child's play and adult joy. And cooking done with care is an act of love." I had already poured lots of love into the Laughing Buddha that I'd prepared for my wife, Felicia, the night we met, but it wasn't because I was hoping for and expecting anything other than I wanted her to enjoy her drink.

Change that. I had hoped that Felicia and every single one of my other guests would absolutely adore and fall in love with their cocktails.

A restaurant's lighting and audio experience are carefully assembled, as are the aesthetics of the room, the selection and arrangement of furniture, the art hung on the walls. Then there is the back bar, a few hundred bottles curated for the public's drinking pleasure. And, of course, the menu, which is hopefully a brilliant, brief piece of writing wholly indicative of the special offerings of the establishment.

As an entrepreneur, I've poured plenty of hours into these decisions and also into the daily interactions with my guests. I've come home from shifts and have been absolutely exhausted, not because I had been on my feet for a dozen very physical hours, but because of all the emotional care I had poured into every single guest, into each guest's drink, and into the many chats across the wood.

My hope is to offer something brilliant yet absolutely personal to every guest. I believe that a great barman must inhabit the creation of every drink, that he or she must birth the liquid in the glass across the bar, thinking, feeling, knowing that this exact drink has never been made before and could, should, will be an unforgettable experience.

Guests often don't know what they like, or perhaps they don't know how to communicate what they do enjoy when they order a cocktail. When this confusing juncture occurs, I typically counter with a sincere, "How was your day?" This old-school barman's psychology serves not only to create a familiar banter with the guest but also to establish a guidepost for the drinking experience about to commence. The opener is followed by a litany of other questions, the most important of which are, "How do you want to feel in fifteen minutes?" "Is there anything you absolutely love or hate?" "Are you allergic to anything, maybe almonds, cinnamon, juniper?"

Nine times out of ten, I end up serving the guest either a perfectly improvised cocktail suited to his or her day or an appropriate classic. I've also learned if a big contract has just been signed and the celebration will go for hours, or if divorce papers have just been filed and the opposite is true. On one occasion, after learning that a guest was in a dark mood and needed a stiff drink to shake off the day, I composed an old fashioned with Qi smoked black tea liqueur and a bright grapefruit (rather than orange) peel. Not only did that drink do the trick but it became his signature cocktail, which he ordered with pride on all of his subsequent visits.

Cocktails are meant to be playful; they should also be served with love. Whether making a drink at home or behind the bar, one may never know what might happen as a result of caring so damn much.

# TO HOLD THE PAST
# IN THE FUTURE

*I read the signs of the times, and I, that am no prophet, behold
the things that are in store for you. Over slumbering California is stealing
the dawn of a radiant future! . . . She stands in the centre of the grand
highway of the nations: she stands midway between the Old world and the
New, and both shall pay her tribute. . . . Half the world stands ready to
lay its contributions at her feet! Has any other State so brilliant a future?
Has any other city a future like San Francisco?*

*This straggling town shall be a vast metropolis: this sparsely
populated land shall become a crowded hive of busy men: your waste places
shall blossom like the rose and your deserted hills and valleys shall yield
bread and wine for unnumbered thousands: railroads shall be spread hither
thither and carry the invigorating blood of commerce to regions
that are languishing now. . . .*

*I am bidding the old city and my old friends a kind, but not a sad farewell,
for I know that when I see this home again, the changes that will have
been wrought upon it will suggest no sentiment of sadness; its estate will be
brighter, happier and prouder a hundred fold than it is this day.
This is its destiny, and in all sincerity I can say, So mote it be!*

—Mark Twain, *Alta California*

San Francisco, mightily inventive and always inclusive, is a passionate place of discovery where all are welcome and all is available. It is full of history, of many quirks and pre-dilections—a boomtown of successes and celebrations. Let's remember this, because doing so will keep San Francisco, San Francisco. This book is meant in part to serve as a reminder of that, as both a bridge to the past and a door opening into the future. It is a call to arms for localism, for San Francisco to cherish itself, to remember its vibrant past, to celebrate its own idiosyncratic culture. It is also a call to arms for the cocktail communities of Seattle and St. Louis, Austin and Los Angeles, Chicago and Miami. Wherever you may be, champion your story.

The writing of this book was possible only after I chose to champion the cause of preserving and promoting the cocktail culture of the City. It required years of surveying, querying whether my many nights behind-the-stick held the same experiences, the same truths for the members of my community. No matter how many questions I asked and how deeply I dug, the answer was always the same: a resounding yes! But it is not only barkeeps who celebrate our historic, vibrant cocktail culture. The interest in cocktails is alive and well in the broader culture of California and, perhaps soon, in every bar in the land. I spoke with hundreds of people about this book, and not just bar folks or California residents. Cocktails and their stories belong to everyone.

Nowadays, a connoisseur can walk into nearly any cocktail bar in America and order a proper Negroni. The mixological talent in this country is at an all-time high, and anyone anywhere can replicate a recipe. My point though, as you've certainly discovered, is that there is a history, a version of truth, a canon of cocktails that are near and dear to the heart of San Francisco. And from that canon emerges a portrait of the City and of the people who live here. Knowing that this canon exists gives us a dosing of pride, kindles a fire in our bellies to keep telling the stories of our tribe.

While surveying the community, I managed to visit quite a few bars and taste many, many cocktails. Hundreds, if not thousands, of uniquely delicious cocktails are being poured throughout the Bay Area every day. To have included all of cocktails would have necessitated a different, yet still worthy, book. To have included the names of the many bars would have been futile. That's because bars exist in a specific time and place; they capture the attention of an era and can usually boast a season of splendor before the sun sets and the crowd moves on. But cocktails are independent, nomadic properties composed of spirit, which live forever.

San Francisco will always be a city that keeps its doors to the world open twenty-four hours a day. It is a community of many cultures smashed together whose long history of drink dates to 1579. It is a robust environ of privilege, and one that will always be wet: San Francisco wouldn't be San Francisco without a cocktail in her hand. This book was very much written for all of her visitors who have come once, twice, maybe a hundred times to her Michelin-starred restaurants and corner saloons and enjoyed one of the City's signature drams. To visit a city and experience it intimately is an unforgettable joy. To have all of that happen from a bar stool, that's when you know you were in San Francisco.

These days, the Devil's Acre is still a sight to behold. You can do so from one of the little tables outside Cafe Zoetrope; enjoy a Negroni, a French 75, or whatever your palate prefers, and take in the view of that historic island across the way. New bars with cocktails at fourteen dollars a slug are going in next to the old bars such as Specs, in between immigrant-owned restaurants with names like Urban Curry and Little Szechuan. Within the Devil's Acre you can buy a baguette and a cannoli. There are clothing boutiques and a recording studio. The peep shows are still there, too, with big neon signs leaning out into Broadway that advertise forbidden delights inside the Garden of Eden. It is a noisy bit of land, bursting with life and drink and story.

Will the mixological saloons of San Francisco return to their roots as a hub of community, a vibrant avenue for the exchange of ideas, the meeting of new persons, the creation and expansion of new communities? I hope so. Tosca Café sits right in the middle of the Devil's Acre, and some of the biggest talents behind-the-stick are working there these days. That can be a distraction, or the drinks that these talented bartenders deliver can serve as a shim, propping up the whole conversation. Not long ago, Jeannette Etheredge said to me, "Tosca was and is always going to be a neighborhood bar. And the neighborhood is San Francisco."

Creating a signature cocktail for a special occasion is a time-tested tradition. That's what coming to the last page of this text deserves: a little drink that manifests the sins and celebrations of a city built on gold, something delicious that could come only from this place, a terroir-driven tipple, lovely, from San Francisco. I imagine a bracing cocktail slowly stirred so as not to bruise the curves of her pot-distilled nature. I must begin with Campo de Encanto's Single Vine Quebranta, strong with a bit of salinity, just like the sea. Pisco, as you recall, was not only the first spirit imbibed in the domain of California in 1579, but also this grape called Quebranta, known to us as the Mission grape, was the source of the state's first distilled spirit. I imagine a bit of Scotch whisky layered in, a tribute to other lands and to the Barbary Coast, an era of many vices, adding notes of honey and heather. Next comes enough of something holy and herbaceous and full of magic to arouse the tongue: yellow Chartreuse. The drink will need something sweet yet feral, such as agave nectar from Mexico but born in cocktails out in the fog at Tommy's. It will also need that necessary note of bitter, and so just a few dashes of orange bitters will do (a type that originated here, as well). As the drink is stirred, but slowly, I imagine enjoying it on days of wind and fog and in the seeming unending romp of San Francisco. Pour the portrait over a single stone of ice made with Hetch Hetchy water, and finish the aria with a broad lemon peel, expressed and then gently tucked in to brighten the lot.

What does the future hold for San Francisco, for her cocktails and their stories? I can be certain of only one thing: Within our little burg of fog and wind are many repositories of charm, and if your drink comes from the hands of a capable barmaid, and is sent across the wood with love, there is surely a promise, a story inside its glass. That's San Francisco. That itself is the promise. San Francisco has and will always be one long, unending romp of bottles popping, the whole of the world coming together in a den of vice and virtue.

With love, I bid you good night, to find for yourself a bright, bitter, and boozy delight.

### Vice & Virtue

*With love from Duggan McDonnell*

2 oz/60 ml Campo de Encanto Dist. RSV Single Vine Quebranta

½ oz/15 ml Islay Scotch whisky

¼ oz/10 ml yellow Chartreuse

¼ oz/10 ml diluted agave nectar (see note, page 143)

2 dashes orange bitters

Expressed lemon peel for garnish

Pour the liquid into a mixing glass, add ice, then stir slowly and with great intent. Strain into a sturdy glass over a single stone of ice, garnish with the lemon peel, and believe.

Telegraph Hill, Historic View, 1890

TELEGRAPH HILL

CONTEMPORARY LOCATION

HISTORIC LOCATION

# SAN FRANCISCO COCKTAIL ROUTE

When you find yourself thirsty and having some free time in this great City, I recommend traversing the storied cocktail route. Locations marked as HISTORIC are venues long shuttered while others are open for business.

Begin your route at the site of Tom Sawyer's historic saloon, The Gotham, and then wind your way to Union Square, then north into the notorious Barbary Coast.

1. The Gotham (Mission & 3rd)

2. The House of Shields (New Montgomery & Stevenson)

3. Palace Hotel (New Montgomery & Market)

4. The Starlight Room (Powell & Sutter)

5. Cantina (Sutter & Mason)

6. Burritt Room + Tavern (Stockton & Sutter)

7. Trader Vic Alley (Post & Taylor)

8. Tiki Bob's (Post & Taylor)

9. Occidental Hotel (Kearny & Washington)

10. Rickhouse (Kearny & Pine)

11. Tadich Grill (California & Battery)

12. Comstock Saloon (Columbus & Pacific)

13. Hotaling Alley (Pacific & Kearny)

14. Bank Exchange Saloon (Montgomery & Washington)

15. House of Pisco, Terrific Street (Pacific & New Montgomery)

16. The Old Ship Saloon (Pacific & Battery)

17. The Saloon (Grant & Fresno)

18. Tosca (Columbus & Broadway)

19. 15 Romolo (Romolo & Broadway)

20. Original Joe's (Union & Stockton)

# RECOMMENDED READING

Abou-Ganim, Tony. *The Modern Mixologist*. Chicago: Surrey Books, 2010.

Anderson, E. N. *Everyone Eats*. New York: New York University Press, 2005.

Asbury, Herbert. *The Barbary Coast: An Informal History of the San Francisco Underground*. New York: Alfred Knopf, 1933.

Bacon, Daniel. *Walking San Francisco on the Barbary Coast Trail*. San Francisco: Quicksilver Press, 2008.

Beattie, Scott. *Artisanal Cocktails*. Berkeley: Ten Speed Press, 2008.

Bergeron, Victor Jules. *Trader Vic's Bartender's Guide*. Edited by Shirley Sarvis. New York: Doubleday, 1972.

Boothby, William T. *"Cocktail Bill" Boothby's World's Drinks and How to Mix Them*. San Francisco: Boothby's World Drinks Co., 1934.

Caen, Herb. *Baghdad by the Bay*. New York: Doubleday, 1949.

Chartier, François. *Tastebuds and Molecules: The Art of Science, Food and Flavor*. Translated by Levi Reiss. Hoboken, New Jersey: Wiley & Sons, 2012.

Conrad, Barnaby. *Name Dropping: Tales from My Barbary Coast Saloon*. New York: HarperCollins West, 1994.

Fisher, M. F. K. *The Art of Eating*. New York: Macmillan, 1990.

Fracchia, Charles A. *When the Water Came Up to Montgomery Street*. Virginia Beach, VA: Donning, 2009.

Germain-Robin, Hubert. *Traditional Distillation: Art & Passion.* Colorado: White Mule Press, 2012.

Haigh, Ted. *Vintage Spirits and Forgotten Cocktails.* Beverly, MA: Quarry Books, 2009.

Hammett, Dashiell. *The Maltese Falcon.* New York: Alfred A. Knopf, 1930.

Hébert, Malcolm R. *California Brandy Drinks.* San Francisco: The Wine Appreciation Guild with the California Brandy Advisory Board, 1981.

Hollinger, Jeff, and Robert Schwartz. *The Art of the Bar: Cocktails Inspired by the Classics.* San Francisco: Chronicle Books, 2006.

Johnson, Byron A., and Sharon Peregrine Johnson. *Wild West Bartender's Bible.* Austin: Texas Monthly Press, 1986.

Johnson, Harry. *New and Improved Bartender's Manual.* Reprinted by John C. Burton. Santa Rosa, CA: Aperitifs Publishing, 2007. First published 1882.

Lloyd, Benjamin E. *Lights and Shades in San Francisco.* Nabu Press public domain reprint, n.d. First published 1876.

Muscatine, Doris. *Old San Francisco: The Biography of a City from Early Days to the Earthquake.* New York: Putnam, 1975.

O'Brien, Robert. *This Is San Francisco.* New York: Whittlesey House, 1948.

Page, Karen. *The Flavor Bible.* New York: Little, Brown, 2008.

Saroyan, William. *The Time of Your Life.* New York: Bloomsbury Methuen Drama, 2008.

Thomas, Jerry. *How to Mix Drinks, or The Bon Vivant's Companion.* New York: Grosset & Dunlap, 1934. First published 1862.

Toro-Lira, Guillermo. *Wings of Cherubs: The Saga of the Rediscovery of Pisco Punch, Old San Francisco's Mystery Drink.* North Charleston, SC: BookSurge, 2007.

Twain, Mark. *Roughing It.* New York: Signet Classics, 2008. First published 1872.

Wondrich, David. *Imbibe!* New York: Penguin, 2007.

*View of San Francisco from Twin Peaks, September 28, 2011*

# ACKNOWLEDGMENTS

This book was written for a reason: Many great barmen have come before me, created, and then published exceptional work. Without their legacy, and the many great writers and media people here in San Francisco, *Drinking the Devil's Acre* would not exist. To each of them, I bear a tremendous gratitude. I must specifically thank the California Historical Society, the Barbary Coast Trail, the San Francisco Public Library, John Burton, Guillermo Toro-Lira, David Wondrich, Martin Cate, and each of the bartenders, distillers, and writers whose ideas and recipes appear in these pages. Thank you to Amy Treadwell for her support and sage advice, and a very special thanks to my business partners for believing in me, my ideas, and my palate. Thanks, too, to each of the bar backs and bartenders with whom I've pounded the mat, shaken tin, and poured an ocean of liquid across the wood—you made it all real. And to my wife, Felicia, whom I met at Cantina on a hurried Thursday eve after serving her a Laughing Buddha, thanks for putting up with me, babe.

# INDEX

## A

Abou-Ganim, Tony, 8, 120, 137, 139
Absinthe Brasserie & Bar, 8, 88, 90, 112, 120, 138, 204–5
Adams, Ian, 157
Africa, Henry, 178, 185, 186, 187, 199, 200
Agave nectar, 145
    Chinese Five-Spice Agave Nectar, 148
Alfred's Steakhouse, 79
Almonds
    orgeat syrup, 55
Amari, 80–81
Anchor Brewing, 8, 107
Anderson, E. N., 19
Armagnac
    Champs-Élysées, 120
    French 75, 155
    Superior Cocktail Brandy, 123
    White Nun, 90
Asbury, Herbert, 7, 11, 17, 201
Averna
    Intercontinental, 83
    Midnight Smash, 225

## B

Baird, Scott, 70
Bamboo Cocktail, 216
Bank Exchange Saloon, 7, 33, 64–65, 68, 140, 156, 171, 200
Bar Agricole, 71, 173
Barbary Coast (cocktail), 211
Barbary Coast (place), 7, 17, 29, 32
Barkeeps
    legendary, 200–201, 204
    traits of, 198–99
Basil Gimlet, 227–28
Beach, Donn, 94, 128, 181
Beattie, Scott, 9
Beef tea, 114
    Bloody Mary, 111

Bergeron, Trader Vic, 7, 53, 54, 56, 93, 94, 95, 138–39, 146, 178, 197, 199, 200
Bermejo, Julio, 22, 143
Bezuidenhout, Jacques, 148, 216
Big 4, 74
Bitters, 103
    Homemade Aromatic Bitters, 104
Blackberries
    Blackberry and Basil Cooler, 188
    Blackberry and Cabernet Caipirinha, 167
Blackbird, 41
Blended spirits, 44–45
    Superior Cocktail Blackstrap Rum, 194
    Superior Cocktail Brandy, 123
    Superior Cocktail French Vermouth, 215
    Superior Cocktail Maguey, 149
    Superior Cocktail Old Tom Gin, 47
    Superior Cocktail Rum, 181
    Superior Cocktail Vermouth, 51
    Superior Cocktail Vodka, 187
    Superior Cocktail Whiskey, 109
Blood and Sand, 207–9
Bloody Mary, 111–13
Bloomfield, April, 79
Blue Ribbon Sour, 173
Bonné, Jon, 138
Boothby, "Cocktail Bill," 7, 19, 38, 44, 69, 100, 102, 107, 126, 153, 200, 216
Boothby Cocktail, 100, 102
Bourbon, 106
    Cherry Bounce, 160
    Kentucky Buck, 197
    Revolver, 102

Superior Cocktail Whiskey, 109
Brandy, 118–19, 122. See also individual brandies
    Meyer Lemon 75, 160
    Missionary's Downfall, 128
    Sangria, 213
    Scorpion Bowl, 93
    Sidecar, 117
    Spanish Coffee, 90
    Superior Cocktail Brandy, 123
    Vieux Carré, 120
Buddha, 28
Buena Vista, 8, 86–87
Burritt Room + Tavern, 27–28
Burton, John C., 8

## C

Cable Car, 120
Cachaça
    Blackberry and Cabernet Caipirinha, 167
    Superior Cocktail Blackstrap Rum, 194
Caen, Herb, 8
Cafe Zoetrope, 32, 242
Caipirinha, Blackberry and Cabernet, 167
Campari, 78–79, 80–81
    Jasmine, 83
    Negroni, 77
    1794 (cocktail), 83
Campbell, Charles, 7, 19
Cantina, 26, 137, 139, 140, 228, 229, 236
Carlson, Erik, 222
Carmen Amaya, 229
Castro, Erick, 197
Cate, Martin, 54, 56, 60
Cecchini, Toby, 139, 140
Champs-Élysées, 120
Chartier, François, 231
Chartreuse, 222
    Champs-Élysées, 120
    Chartreuse Swizzle, 221–22, 224

Last Word, 211
Misdemeanor, 71
Vice & Virtue, 243
Cherry Bounce, 160
Chinese Five-Spice Agave
 Nectar, 148
Christiansen, Carl, 135, 227,
 228
Churchill, Winston, 37, 38
Citrus, 121, 183
Claiborne, Craig, 238
Cocktail menus, 166
Cocktail syrup, 58–59
Coffee, 88–89
 Cold Brew Coffee Syrup, 91
 Irish Coffee, 85–87
 Spanish Coffee, 88–90
 White Nun, 90
Coffee liqueur
 Revolver, 102
 Spanish Coffee, 90
 White Nun, 90
Cognac
 Dead Reckoning, 56
 House-Made Vanilla-
  Cognac Cordial, 57
 Intercontinental, 83
 Superior Cocktail Brandy,
  123
Cointreau
 Carmen Amaya, 229
 Jasmine, 83
Cold Brew Coffee Syrup, 91
Comstock Saloon, 38, 40, 41,
 50, 156, 160, 208, 209
Cormican, Karri, 208
Corpse Reviver #2, 211
Cox, Jennings, 177, 179
Craddock, Harry, 173, 207
Crème de cacao
 Barbary Coast, 211
Crocker, Charles, 74
Curaçao
 Cable Car, 120
 Champs-Élysées, 120
 Corpse Reviver #2, 211
 Jasmine, 83

Lemon Drop, 185
Mai Tai, 53
Sidecar, 117

**D**
D'Agostino, Paul, 135
Daiquiri, 177–79, 183
Dark 'n Stormy, 191–93
Dead Reckoning, 56
Delaplane, Stan, 85, 87
Dempsey, Jack, 156
Denton, Harry, 8, 137, 140,
 178, 200
Devil's Acre, 11, 17, 32, 40,
 242
Dionysos, Marco, 8, 137, 200,
 203, 204–5, 221, 222
Dirty Habit, 148
Distillery No. 209, 9, 42–43
Dr. T, 216
Drake, Sir Francis, 6, 38, 68,
 125, 128, 129–30, 164
Draquecito, 128, 129, 130

**E**
East India Cocktail, 71
Edison, Thomas, 66
Eggs, 174–75
 Blue Ribbon Sour, 173
 Pisco Sour, 169–72, 174–75
 Rattlesnake, 173
 Silver Fizz, 173
Ehrmann, H. Joseph, 9, 152
El Diablo, 197
Elixir, 152
Enrico's Sidewalk Café, 83,
 126, 127
Eppinger, Louis, 216
Etheredge, Jeannette, 79, 242

**F**
Fairmont Hotel, 94, 95
Farley, Johnny, 153
Farmers' markets, 126, 131
Fernet-Branca, 80–81
15 Romolo, 57, 157
Fisher, M. F. K., 238

Five-Spice Margarita, 148
Fleming, Ian, 38
Fogcutter, 56
Fraser, Mike, 113
French 75, 155–57, 161

**G**
Gentleman's Delight, 105
Gill Sans, 41
Gin, 42–43
 Barbary Coast, 211
 Basil Gimlet, 227
 Corpse Reviver #2, 211
 Fogcutter, 56
 French 75, 155
 Gentleman's Delight, 105
 Gill Sans, 41
 Ginger Rogers, 203
 Jasmine, 83
 Last Word, 211
 Laura Palmer, 41
 Marguerite, 41
 Martinez, 37
 Negroni, 77
 Silver Fizz, 173
 Superior Cocktail Old Tom
  Gin, 47
Ginger beer, 196
 Blackberry and Basil Cooler,
  188
 Dark 'n Stormy, 191
 El Diablo, 197
 Kentucky Buck, 197
 Laughing Buddha, 235–37
 Midnight Smash, 225
 Moscow Mule, 197
Ginger Rogers, 203–5
Gum arabic, 69
 Gum Arabic Cordial, 70
**H**
Hammett, Dashiell, 27
Harrington, Paul, 8, 83
Harry's New York Bar, 112,
 118, 119, 156–57
Heering cherry liqueur
 Blood and Sand, 207–9
Helper, Hinton, 29

Hemingway (cocktail), 180
Hemingway, Ernest, 156, 180
Henry Africa's, 8, 178, 185, 186, 200
Herbért, Malcolm, 119
Hetch Hetchy Reservoir, 217–18
Highball, 73–74
Hillesland, Arne, 42–43
Hobday, Norman. *See* Africa, Henry
Hocker, Curtis, 8
Hollinger, Jeff, 9, 41, 50
Hopkins, Mark, 74
Hotaling, A. P., 33
Huntington, Collis, 74
Huntington Hotel, 74
The Hut, 95

**I**
Ice, 218
Intercontinental, 83
Intermezzo, 216
Irish whiskey
    Irish Coffee, 85
Irwin, Inez Haynes, 16
Iverson, John R., 7

**J**
Jacobson, Pauline, 64, 65
Jasmine, 83
Johnson, Harry, 7, 19, 21, 38, 41, 69, 71, 118, 139–40, 163, 164, 165, 171, 173, 177, 179, 180, 199, 200–201, 213, 214
Josie, Brandon, 57

**K**
Kelly, "Shanghai," 199
Kent, Frances, 78–79
Kentucky Buck, 197
Kipling, Rudyard, 65
Koeppler, Jack, 85, 87
Kosevich, Nick, 103

**L**
La Perla, 148
Last Word, 211
Laughing Buddha, 235–37
Laura Palmer, 41
Lazar, Michael, 9
Lefty O'Doul's, 113
Lemon Drop, 185–86
Leo XIII (pope), 66
Lillet Blanc
    Corpse Reviver #2, 211
    Laura Palmer, 41
Lillet Rouge, 66
Lindgren, Greg, 227, 228
Li Po, 28
Lloyd, Benjamin, 17

**M**
MacElhone, Harry, 112, 117, 118, 155, 156
Mackay, Jordan, 9, 229
Maher, Jane, 86
Mai Tai, 28, 53–54
Manhattan, 99–101
Maraschino liqueur
    Gill Sans, 41
    Hemingway, 180
    Intercontinental, 83
    Last Word, 211
    Martinez, 37
    Prize Filly, 102
    Superior Cocktail Vodka, 187
Margarita, 143–45
    Five-Spice Margarita, 148
Marguerite, 41
Mariani, Angelo, 66
Marshall, Ian, 99
Martinez, 37–38, 40
Martini, 38
Maytag, Fritz, 8, 107
MECCA, 134–36, 137, 222, 228
Menus, 166
Meyer lemons, 158
    Meyer Lemon Marmalade, 159

Meyer Lemon 75, 160
Mezcal
    Chinese Five-Spice Agave Nectar, 148
    Single Village Fix, 71
    Superior Cocktail Maguey, 149
Midnight Smash, 225
Misdemeanor, 71
Missionary's Downfall, 128
Mojito, 125–27, 129–30
Morris, Victor, 169, 171
Morris Bar, 171
Morss, Karen, 158, 159
Moscow Mule, 197
Muir, John, 217, 218
Munat, Ted, 9
Muscatine, Doris, 25
Mystic Hotel, 27

**N**
Negroni, 77–79
Negroni, Count Camillo, 77
Nepove, David, 125, 126–27
Nicol, Duncan, 7, 33, 63, 64–65, 66, 68, 69, 140, 156, 199, 200
NoMad, 83

**O**
Occidental Hotel, 6, 40
Odeon, 140
Old Ship Saloon, 6
Orgeat syrup, 54, 55
Original Joe's, 113

**P**
Palace Hotel, 100, 101
Passerby, 140
Pear liqueur
    La Perla, 148
Peerless Saloon, 151, 153
Petiot, Fernand "Pete," 111, 112
Petri, Art, 79
Peychaud, Antoine, 151
Pied Piper, 100, 101

Pier 23 Cafe, 192
Pimm's Cup, 225
Pineapple, 69
  Chartreuse Swizzle, 221
  East India Cocktail, 71
  Homemade Pineapple
    Cordial, 70
  Misdemeanor, 71
  Missionary's Downfall, 128
  Pisco Punch, 63
  Single Village Fix, 71
Pink Door, 100–101
Pisco, 67–68, 129–30
  Blue Ribbon Sour, 173
  Draquecito, 128
  East India Cocktail, 71
  Fogcutter, 56
  Pisco Punch, 63–66
  Pisco Sour, 169–72, 174–75
  Superior Cocktail Vodka,
    187
  Vice & Virtue, 243
Pizarro, Francisco, 67, 129
Port
  Dead Reckoning, 56
Prizefighter, 102
Prize Filly, 102

R
Raglin, Jonny, 160
Rattlesnake, 173
Regan, Gaz, 9, 78, 138, 140
Revolver, 102
Rickhouse, 197
Rum, 60–61, 130
  Cable Car, 120
  Daiquiri, 177
  Dark 'n Stormy, 191
  Dead Reckoning, 56
  East India Cocktail, 71
  Fogcutter, 56
  Hemingway, 180
  Homemade Aromatic
    Bitters, 104
  Mai Tai, 53
  Missionary's Downfall, 128
  Mojito, 125

St. Croix Rum Punch, 180
Sangria, 213
Scorpion Bowl, 93
Spanish Coffee, 90
Superior Cocktail Blackstrap
  Rum, 194
Superior Cocktail Rum, 181
Wilson's Smash, 57
Rumbustion Society, 60–61
Russo, Charlie, 41
Rye (bar), 228
Rye whiskey, 107
  Carmen Amaya, 229
  Manhattan, 99
  Prize Filly, 102
  Rattlesnake, 173
  Sazerac, 151
  1794 (cocktail), 83
  Superior Cocktail Whiskey,
    109
  Vieux Carré, 120

S
St. Croix Rum Punch, 180
Sanchez, Felicia, 236–37,
  238–39
Sanchez, Michael, 78–79
San Francisco
  cocktail culture of, 17–23,
    29, 32–33, 138
  Cocktail Route, 246–47
  future of, 240–43
  history of, 6–9, 16–17, 18,
    20, 29
  liquor licenses in, 17
  tea and coffee in, 81
Sangria, 213–14
Santer, Jon, 102
Saroyan, William, 7, 32, 198
Savoy Hotel, 207
Sawyer, Tom, 33, 63
Sazerac, 151–53
Scarselli, Fosco, 77
Schwartz, Robert, 9
Scorpion Bowl, 93–95, 97
Scotch
  Barbary Coast, 211

Blood and Sand, 207–9
Dr. T, 216
Scotch and Soda, 73–74
Vice & Virtue, 243
Serra, Father Junípero, 20
1794 (cocktail), 83
Sharing, 97
Sherry
  Bamboo Cocktail, 216
  Blue Ribbon Sour, 173
  Carmen Amaya, 229
  Fogcutter, 56
  Gill Sans, 41
  La Perla, 148
  Superior Cocktail Brandy,
    123
  Superior Cocktail French
    Vermouth, 215
  Superior Cocktail Old Tom
    Gin, 47
Shoemaker, Daniel, 55, 136–
  37, 204
Shumway, Isaac, 90
Sidecar, 117–19
Silver Fizz, 173
Simonson, Robert, 78
Simple syrup, 58–59
Single Village Fix, 71
Sir Francis Drake Hotel, 8, 27
Smash, 163–65
Smuggler's Cove, 54, 60–61
Southworth, May E., 7
Spanish Coffee, 88–90
Stanford, Leland, 74
Starlight Room, 8, 27, 120,
  137, 200, 204, 216, 222
Stars, 205
Stenson, Murray, 22
Sutton, Carl, 49–50
Sutton Cellars, 49–50

T
Tasting, 231–33
Teardrop Lounge, 55, 136
Tequila, 146–47
  Dr. T, 216
  El Diablo, 197

Five-Spice Margarita, 148
La Perla, 148
Margarita, 143
Misdemeanor, 71
Superior Cocktail Maguey,
    149
ThirstyBear Brewing Company,
    136–37
Thomas, Jerry, 6, 19, 21, 29,
    37, 38, 40, 126, 138,
    199, 200–201
Tomato juice
    Bloody Mary, 111
Tommy's Mexican Restaurant,
    8, 22, 143–45, 242
Tonga Room, 94, 95, 97
Toro-Lira, Guillermo, 9
Tosca Café, 79, 89, 90, 242
Trader Vic's Restaurant, 7, 60
Trick Dog, 70
Twain, Mark, 7, 33, 63, 240

**V**
Vecchio, Rick, 171
Velvet Falernum liqueur
    Chartreuse Swizzle, 221
Venegas, Dominic, 83
Vera, Nico, 172
Vermouth, 49–50
    Bamboo Cocktail, 216
    Blood and Sand, 207–9
    Boothby Cocktail, 102
    Gentleman's Delight, 105
    Manhattan, 99
    Marguerite, 41
    Martinez, 37
    Negroni, 77
    Prize Filly, 102
    Sangria, 213
    1794 (cocktail), 83
    Superior Cocktail French
        Vermouth, 215
    Superior Cocktail Vermouth,
        51
    Vieux Carré, 120
Vesuvio Cafe, 8

Vice & Virtue, 243
Vieux Carré, 120
Vin Mariani, 66
Vodka, 38
    Blackberry and Basil Cooler,
        188
    Bloody Mary, 111
    Laughing Buddha, 235–37
    Lemon Drop, 185
    Midnight Smash, 225
    Moscow Mule, 197
    Superior Cocktail Vodka,
        187
Vogler, Thad, 71, 173

**W**
Washington, George, 106
Water
    importance of, 218
    sparkling, 75
Whiskey, 106–7. *See also*
    Bourbon; Irish whiskey; Rye
        whiskey; Scotch
    Boothby Cocktail, 102
    Homemade Aromatic
        Bitters, 104
    Superior Cocktail Whiskey,
        109
White Nun, 89, 90
Wilson's Smash, 57
Wine, 214
    Blackberry and Cabernet
        Caipirinha, 167
    Boothby Cocktail, 102
    Cherry Bounce, 160
    Corpse Reviver #2, 211
    Dr. T, 216
    French 75, 155
    Intermezzo, 216
    Meyer Lemon 75, 160
    Pisco Punch, 63
    Sangria, 213
    sparkling, 161
    Superior Cocktail French
        Vermouth, 215
    Superior Cocktail Vermouth,
        51

**Y**
Yosemite National Park, 217,
    218

**Z**
Zig Zag Café, 211
Zuni Café, 113

## DUGGAN McDONNELL

# RULES FOR BUDDING
# BARMEN AND YOUNG MIXOLOGISTS
# EVERYWHERE

1. The customer is not always right; rather, the customer is a guest of the bar, and as your bar is the veritable home of you the bartender, do everything to make your guest feel at home. You the bartender may be part psychiatrist, chef, tour guide, confidante, coconspirator, and master of ceremonies. Yet none of your efforts will matter if your guest ceases to be your focus.

2. Wash your hands often.

3. Great experiences can be had in bars without imbibing a drop of alcohol. Remember this when a guest arrives to sit on your bar stool.

4. Wipe down your bar top constantly, not leaving a bit of moisture or a tiny puddle for your guest to accidentally sink his or her sleeve or elbow into.

5. A delicious cocktail is a balanced cocktail.

6. Human beings love the sound of their names more than any song. At every opportunity, affirm the importance of your guests by addressing each of them by name.

7. Taste and smell every bottle and every drink you serve across your bar to ensure its freshness, its balance, and that it is, in fact, what your guest called for.

8. Entertaining your guests with your movements—the beautiful ballet-meets-trench-warfare of a busy cocktail bar—is your duty. Your guests have indeed come to see you twirl and move. Don't forget to serve them their drinks.

9. Human contact will never lose its importance; lightly returning your guest's change to her hand after a transaction, while maintaining eye contact and sincerely saying "thank you," may in fact be more of a reward than her painstakingly stirred cocktail and will certainly boost your gratuities.

10. It's a fine tradition for you to have a drink with your guests or with a fellow barkeep. Simply remember that you may still have many hours to go until you've finished cleaning the bar, balancing the receipts, and locking the front door before you should fully relax. Keep your wits about you.